Edwin Abbott Abbott, Arthur Sidgwick, Henry Weston Eve

Three lectures on subjects connected with the practice of education; delivered in the University of Cambridge in the Easter term, 1882

Edwin Abbott Abbott, Arthur Sidgwick, Henry Weston Eve

Three lectures on subjects connected with the practice of education; delivered in the University of Cambridge in the Easter term, 1882

ISBN/EAN: 9783337214845

Printed in Europe, USA, Canada, Australia, Japan

Cover: Foto ©Paul-Georg Meister /pixelio.de

More available books at **www.hansebooks.com**

Pitt Press Series.

THREE LECTURES

ON SUBJECTS CONNECTED WITH

THE PRACTICE OF EDUCATION

DELIVERED IN THE UNIVERSITY OF CAMBRIDGE
IN THE EASTER TERM, 1882,

BY

H. W. EVE, M.A.
HEAD MASTER OF UNIVERSITY COLLEGE SCHOOL;

ARTHUR SIDGWICK, M.A.
FELLOW AND TUTOR OF CORPUS CHRISTI COLLEGE, OXFORD, AND LATE ASSISTANT MASTER AT RUGBY SCHOOL;

AND

E. A. ABBOTT, M.A. D.D.
HEAD MASTER OF THE CITY OF LONDON SCHOOL.

Cambridge:
AT THE UNIVERSITY PRESS.

London: C. J. CLAY, M.A. & SON,
CAMBRIDGE UNIVERSITY PRESS WAREHOUSE,
17, PATERNOSTER ROW.
1883

[*All Rights reserved.*]

PREFACE.

THE three lectures contained in this volume were delivered by their authors at the request of the Teachers Training Syndicate. The University of Cambridge determined about four years ago to institute lectures on and to hold examinations in the History, Theory and Practice of Education. For the first two years, complete courses of lectures on the Practice of Education were delivered by Mr J. G. Fitch, and Canon Daniel. After this, it seemed to the Syndicate better to revert to a plan originally proposed, and to ask distinguished teachers to deliver single lectures on subjects with which they were specially familiar.

The lectures here presented excited much interest and attention when they were first heard in the University. It has been thought that their publication will make them accessible to a wider circle, and may help to stimulate the movement towards the systematic training of teachers, which is every day assuming larger proportions.

OSCAR BROWNING.

KING'S COLLEGE, CAMBRIDGE,
January, 1883.

CONTENTS.

	PAGE
ON MARKING, BY H. W. EVE, M.A.	1
ON STIMULUS, BY ARTHUR SIDGWICK, M.A.	29
ON THE TEACHING OF LATIN VERSE COMPOSITION, BY E. A. ABBOTT, D.D.	67

ON MARKING.

By H. W. EVE, M.A.
HEAD MASTER OF UNIVERSITY COLLEGE SCHOOL.

ON MARKING[1].

WHEN your Syndicate did me the honour of asking me to lecture before you, I thought I could not do better than select a plain every-day subject, which must take up a good deal of a schoolmaster's time and attention, however little it may, at first, attract his real interest. Whether the element of constant competition, which plays so important a part in English education, is altogether good, I do not propose to discuss; the whole question of "Stimulus" will fall into abler hands than mine. It is, at least, the system under which most of us have to work, and whether good marking be superfluous or not, no one will deny that slovenly and inefficient marking is detrimental. Justice is, perhaps, the quality which most of all commends itself to the young; and injustice at school, as elsewhere, is more frequently due to ignorance or carelessness than to partiality. I have no intention, however, of embarking on so wide a subject as justice at school, at the risk of having to imitate Plato, and to construct an ideal school to illustrate my definition. I propose to deal with only a small portion of school administration, but I hope at the same time to suggest some thoughts on the graver aspects of our profession. If my remarks seem somewhat common-place, I can only plead

[1] Reprinted by permission from the *Journal of Education*.

that nearly every point on which I shall dwell has been raised by difficulties occurring within my own experience. Many of my conclusions will be self-evident to any one accustomed to think in numbers, as I hold every school-master should be. In fact, I should be disposed, for many reasons, to write over the door of the profession a sort of Μηδεὶς ἀγεωμέτρητος εἰσίτω, and to require a saving knowledge of arithmetic as an indispensable condition of entry.

It will be convenient to discuss, first, the marking of paper-work, including both examination-papers and the exercises and translations occurring in our daily routine; next, ordinary class-marking; and lastly, the reduction and combination of marks.

First, then, an exercise or translation may be marked in three different ways. You may subdivide it into a number of small problems, and give marks for everything that is right—which I would call the *constructive* method of marking; or, you may deduct for mistakes from a given maximum, which we will call the *destructive* method; or, lastly, you may mark by general impression without going consciously into details. There are many kinds of work, but mostly beyond the range of school routine, to which the last method alone is applicable; I would only say that it is not easy to mark in a very trustworthy way from impression without some preliminary discipline in marking in detail.

The second, or destructive, method is perhaps the commonest in school-work. In its most primitive form it consists in accepting a maximum assigned by the authorities, and deducting one for each mistake. I do not suppose that any of those whom I have the honour of addressing, would fall into quite such a helpless system; but it is convenient to take an extreme case, if only for the sake of pointing out one or two common errors in marking. Why, then, is the plan I have mentioned so obviously absurd? First, it is clear that there are mistakes and mistakes: one mistake may involve a total misconception of the meaning of a passage, or a gross violation of a grammatical principle,— another may consist in the ignorance of an accessory word, or a trivial blunder in orthography; one may be a failure in reasoning,—the other a mere deficiency in verbal memory. No reasonable person would put the spelling of *adresser* with two *d*'s on a level with *il a se levé*, or an error in the gender of *porticus* or *silex* with *ut* and a subjunctive after a verb of declaring.

Or, again, let us take a short sentence of French. The author has been speaking of the resemblance between men and animals, and continues,—" Enfin il n'est jusqu'au langage qui ne semble commun à l'homme et à l'animal, car on peut voir les animaux s'entendre et se concerter par des signes dont le sens se devine aux mouvements qui les suivent." The first line, you will see, or you would see if you were accustomed to teach average boys, is easily misunderstood. Half the class will make out that language is *not* common to men and to animals, and lose themselves in a delightful *non-sequitur*. Now, that is just the mistake I should mark most severely. If 10 marks were given for the whole passage, 5 of them would be ruthlessly cut off, while a minor error, a mis-translation say of *se concerter*, would forfeit only 1 or 2. And, apropos of this short quotation, I would point out, that in selecting extracts for examination nothing is so important as to choose passages where the general sense is a guide for those who catch it, and a convenient *reductio ad absurdum* for those who do not. This is especially necessary in French, where so much is really easy that the disciplinary value of translation is at times in danger of being lost. *En revanche*, I have heard a distinguished schoolmaster say that he could always catch his Sixth tripping in Guizot.

But to return to our marking: the primitive plan I have mentioned errs in another way. Suppose you reckon, whether rationally or irrationally, 25 mistakes, and deduct them. If your standard is 50, the paper will have 25, and come out as an average production; if your standard is 100, it will have 75, and be reckoned decidedly good. Or, to put it more strongly, suppose you reckon 50 mistakes, the difference, according as you choose for your standard 100 or 50, is that between an average exercise and an absolutely worthless one. It is clear, then, that there comes a point at which we must say to ourselves,—Such and such an exercise is an average one for the class, and must be marked accordingly; such another is poor, but not absolutely worthless, and so on. You must, in fact, *think in numbers* for some of your exercises; the rest of the set can then be treated more mechanically. I believe there is something fascinating in the practice of thinking in numbers, —at least if I may credit a story I once heard of two young schoolmasters. They had been spending their holidays, as young schoolmasters mostly do, in Switzerland, and were passing through Paris on the way home. Other topics failing, they took to *marking* their friends for intellectual power, manners, temper, and what not. At last they went so far as to apply their numerical gauge to the personal appearance of the ladies they met, and it is recorded that, on one whispering to the other 17 (20 was the maximum), they followed a carriage at a respectful distance all the way to the Arc de Triomphe, and missed their train in consequence. Seriously, there are few faculties that a schoolmaster should cultivate more than the critical faculty—the delicate discrimination of degrees of merit, not merely as between boy and boy, but with reference to an ideal standard. And the habit of discrimination in details is no bad training for the higher kind of discrimination, which not only enables a schoolmaster to deal wisely with boys in difficult cases, but also often makes him the most competent adviser as to their future.

But I fear I have digressed rather too far: the two points I have wished to bring out are—(1) that mistakes are of very unequal value: and (2) that, whatever mechanical routine you adopt, your results ought to conform to your general impression. My own plan in marking a set of exercises for examination, if I want to keep the papers themselves intact, is to lay a sheet of paper with vertical divisions beside the exercises, and enter my deductions for each boy in a separate column—5 for a bad mistake, 1 for a trivial one, and so on, and here and there a +2 or +5, if I see any extra good turn. The advantage of the sheet of paper is that, if I forget what value I assigned to a given mistake, or change my mind, I can at once refer to the column. Then I proceed to choose my maximum. Suppose, for example, the best exercise has 20 to be deducted, the worst 70. Suppose I think, too, that the worst exercise deserves some marks, and that the best is good, but not brilliant; I choose 80 for my maximum, thus giving 60 to the best and 10 to the worst, and the others fall into their places between. If I still thought there was room for improvement—if, for example, I thought the best exercise was inadequately remunerated with $\frac{3}{4}$ marks,—I could easily add, say, 10 marks to the best, and a proportionate amount, in this case $\frac{1}{6}$, to the other. The reduction or raising to the standard assigned by external authority is a matter of simple arithmetic.

With regard to the *constructive* method of marking such a piece, it is often a useful check on the *destructive* method to apply it to two or three exercises, especially if, as will sometimes happen, the exercise is rather too hard for the class. I should be disposed to apply the *constructive* method at the two ends of the scale,—on the one hand, to a very bad set of exercises, and, on the other, to more advanced composition, where mistakes are few, and style and turning the most important thing. It is the natural way, for example, of looking over prize translations, at any rate into prose. But I should be sorry to dogmatize on methods, —everyone in the long run makes his method for himself; I am chiefly concerned to urge the importance of making that method represent, both in its details and its general result, one's deliberate judgment on boys' performances,— of using a system of marks, in fact, as one's servant, and not as one's master.

In this connection, I should like to notice one effectual means of promoting good marking, because it suggests a way of gaining experience otherwise than from failure—I mean the practice adopted in many of the Public Schools of examining in committee, so that the same exercise is submitted to two examiners. It causes double trouble, it is true, at a busy time; at the same time it not only minimizes the risk of error, but also affords an invaluable opportunity to a novice of learning from a more experienced hand, and gives to even experienced hands a chance of profiting by each other's experience. I do not think we are quite alive to the danger a schoolmaster incurs of getting into a groove, and not producing his best; his work is mostly lonely, criticised only by immature minds, whose criticism rarely reaches him; it is utterly different from the perpetual conflict of the bar, or the give-and-take of the scientific world. Young men, living together in a common room, do stir each other up: for those of us who have grown older, and live more apart, there is often little left but to apply, in a humble way, such maxims as Lord Bacon suggests in his Essay of Great Place—for example, "Examine thyself strictly whether thou didst not best at first."

Before I leave Language-teaching, I will say a few words about the marking of a complete paper, say on a book of Virgil or a play of Schiller. Suppose it is for a middle form, and contains a couple of passages of 12 or 14 lines for translation, several detached lines for translation and explanation, one or two general questions, and some straight-forward parsing. First of all, never mind about the maximum—that will take care of itself. *Your* maximum can always be reduced or raised. Pick out first the easiest question, say the parsing of a case of a noun, to which you might assign 2 or 3 or 4,—1 or 2 for the case, the number, and gender, 1 or 2 for the reason of its case. By the way, never assign 1 to any question, unless it be such a simple question as "What is the supine of *pello*," which must be absolutely right or absolutely wrong. Otherwise, you will have fractions, which are in all cases to be eschewed. Next, for the isolated scraps. As they are chosen for their difficulty, probably none is worth less than 5, the explanation attached to each will carry from 2 to 5, or even more. And mind that, in setting the paper, you make it clear what explanation you want. Again, there are explanations and explanations. If you ask for the explanation of the subjunctive in "*Socrates accusatus est quod corrumperet juventutem*," you will give something to the boy who says it is a case of virtual oblique oration; you will give a good deal more to one who takes it step by step, and tells you—"(1) They said—'Socrates is worthy of blame, because he corrupts the young;' (2) they said that Socrates was worthy of blame because he corrupted the young; (3) 'they said that Socrates was worthy of blame' is represented by 'Socrates was accused'." Going on in this way, you will find that your *pièces de résistance*, the continuous passages, will require some 40 or 50 marks each. Of the method of marking such pieces, I have already said enough. I would only repeat that errors in these must be marked as severely as errors in the isolated passages, fives being deducted pretty freely; and that a translation where all the points are missed, should have absolutely nothing, even though two or three easy lines are rendered correctly. And do not forget to allow some marks for style. To put the case a little differently—what you really have to estimate is, not the excess of a boy's knowledge over absolute zero, but its excess over what may be called the light of nature. In a general public examination, some credit may reasonably be given for the knowledge even of detached words and phrases; in the examination in prepared work of a class supposed to be reading a book within their comprehension, such knowledge means nothing, and your marks should tell an idle boy plainly that you think so. I need hardly say that a paper should be *set* with this principle clearly in one's mind.

In looking over papers where the answers are in the form of short essays, narratives, or explanations, as in the case of History or Science papers, it is not easy to give rules, and much must be left to general impression.

A lucid answer, hitting all the points, is of course the ideal, and such an answer is sure to get justice done to it. It is generally worth while not to treat the answer *en bloc*, but to make up your mind what are the several points you expect, and assign part of your marks to each, with a pretty wide margin for general effect. One great danger is, lest a clumsy answer, correct in the main points, should be undermarked, especially if, as is often the case, bad writing goes with ill-arranged thought. A careless or inexperienced examiner will not always take the trouble to follow a boy's train of thought, and may do serious injustice. The ill-expressed answer *may* be the result of genuine assimilation of an idea; a more lucid one *may* be merely glib reproduction. Nothing in the course of teaching has given me greater pleasure, than to find that when, for example, I have done a series of experiments and talked about them, several boys have written substantially correct accounts of them, but all in different words. I should be sorry to undervalue the faculty of accurate reproduction, and stigmatize it as "cram"; but I should still press for great care in judging the genuine workings of an immature mind, when you are lucky enough to get them. One word more as to History papers. It is needless to say that your questions will probably be of unequal values, and that you will not find out their true relative values till you have looked over several papers. But there is no subject in which examiners are fonder of setting *alternative* questions, often ridiculously unequal. Thus you will see short biographies of half-a-dozen statesmen in one question, and an account of the Gunpowder Plot, in another, carrying, as alternatives, the same marks. The best remedy is to arrange your alternative questions in groups of two or three;

it is easy to make two or three questions practically equal, but almost impossible to equalize a dozen.

Next, one or two hints as to marking Arithmetic, both in daily work and in examinations. No one of any experience goes simply by the answer, but it is reasonable to condemn at once a gross absurdity, as when an ordinary drawing-room requires 100,000 yards of paper, or a pipe of Johannisberg costs 5s. 6d. In teaching, one sometimes tries to counteract such blind proceedings, by making boys write down rough answers before they begin the formal working, and this is one of the best kinds of mental arithmetic. If the answer is wrong, but not unreasonable, it is well to allow a good deal for method, and to hunt down the mistake, even at the cost of a little extra trouble. If you think how many operations have to be performed in even a simple sum, it is easy to see that a child may easily be discouraged if this be neglected. Verbal explanations, too, should be encouraged; I generally put at the head of an Arithmetic paper a maxim very inapplicable to most things in this world, "Use as many *words* as possible;" for it is only by the free use of words that Arithmetic becomes a training in methodical reasoning.

Before I leave the marking of paper work, I should like to notice a plan adopted in the South Kensington examinations[1], which is very suggestive. A South Kensington examination generally involves the marking, in a limited time, of 3,000 or 4,000 sets of answers to the same questions. There is a chief examiner, who sets the paper and looks over the very best answers, and three or four sub-examiners,

---

[1] It is worth mentioning that the Civil Service Commission require each examiner to send in complete answers to his own paper, a most useful check.

who do the bulk of the work. It is, of course, of great importance to secure uniformity, and they proceed as follows:—The examiners meet, talk over the paper, learn what answers the chief expects, and assign their marks. Then each of the sub-examiners looks over say fifty or sixty of his thousand, marks them, and notes all the difficulties that occur. Truth, some philosophers say, is one; be that as it may, error is undoubtedly various, and in this process unexpected forms of error are certain to crop up. Thus prepared, the examiners meet again, and discuss the vagaries they have encountered. Then they return to their duties with a revised scale of marking, and, it is to be hoped, attain something like uniformity of standard. Now, to look over a thousand sets of answers to the same paper by people you don't care about, is next door to penal servitude; but the process is instructive to those of us whose tasks are more limited and more interesting. However carefully one gets up a paper before looking it over, it is impossible either to anticipate all the more or less distant approximations to correctness you will meet with, or to estimate their value; and therefore I should recommend every one to keep his standard a little elastic till the first four or five papers are done, to note his details in an accessible form, and then to go back and revise his scale of marks. One finds it necessary in looking over any but a quite elementary set of school exercises.

Next, let us pass to Class-marking, or the record of the result of daily lessons,—an operation to which I confess I attach more importance than is, perhaps, now the fashion. The healthy reaction against what Lord Byron calls—

"The drill'd dull lesson, forced down word by word,
 In my repugnant youth,"

has led some people to an opposite extreme, and induced them to dwell on the communication of knowledge by the teacher, rather than on its acquisition by the pupil, and therefore to depreciate the machinery for exacting mental effort, in comparison with the methods for presenting information. I know how much most of us have to learn in the latter direction; to-day I am confining myself to a humbler task. I want to answer the question, How can one best utilise the principle of emulation, in order that as many as possible of a class may, from day to day, really exert themselves to master their lesson? Political economists, pure and simple, conceive mankind as animated by the one desire of buying in the cheapest and selling in the dearest market; they find that it conduces to clearness of thought to eliminate for the time all other motives. In the same way, to compare small things with great, I should like, for the nonce, to think of a boy simply as a creature desirous of marks, and his teacher as the just distributor of them. We are all agreed that there are nobler and better motives to study, but we are not more likely to commend those higher motives to our pupils, if we mark in a casual, slovenly, half-hearted way. Careless marking often means the discouragement of merit, and the tacit approval of idleness.

One naturally touches first on the time-honoured system of Place-taking—the plan according to which a question is passed down from boy to boy, and the one who answers it goes above all who have missed. It has in its favour its liveliness and excitement, a certain amount of rough justice, and, I think, a general popularity with boys. Against it are to be urged the gambling element involved, and the danger of discouraging slow but sound learners. Some would add, that it affords opportunity for noise and confusion, and delays work. It does, no doubt, add to the difficulties of a weak disciplinarian. To any such I would recommend, first, to see that the material arrangements are good, and next, if there is any disorder associated with place-taking, to discontinue it for a time as a punishment. Be that as it may, we may assume that place-taking is an institution, and say a few words as to how it may be most effectively worked. I will begin with describing its worst possible form. I have heard of a class arranged alphabetically at the beginning of a month, in which, at the end of that month, the original order, the ὄνειδος σπαργάνων, was traceable, not only in the total, but in the places the boys actually occupied. Everyone remembers the story Sir Walter Scott tells of his own school-days, how there was one boy at the head of the class whom he could not displace by fair means, and how he finally superseded him by cutting off the button unconsciously associated with all his mental operations. Had the Dominie understood marking, Sir Walter would have been spared the temptation. There is another extreme. You may concentrate all your energies on place-taking, and cease to instruct,—which is indeed "propter vitam vivendi perdere causas". It is necessary, on the one hand, to treat the change of places only as an accessory of teaching, and, on the other, to make it impossible for a boy to feel that he has no chance of getting up, however well he may learn his lesson. The ideal would, no doubt, be to arrange one's class every day in strict order of merit; but that is almost out of the question, and boys are quick enough to see the conditions of the game. They can easily bear, and ought to learn to bear, small disappointments, just as a rising cricketer is not, if he has anything in him, discouraged by one or two unsuccessful innings. I will give a few hints. First, as to the physical conditions.

Perhaps the best plan is for the boys to be sitting, or occasionally standing, round the wall of the room. But, for much of their work, they ought to be sitting in rows in front of the master, with the light coming from the left-hand side; and few people are fortunate enough to have a very large room, or a double set of seats. If they take places in their ordinary rows, it is, on the whole, best to arrange them at the successive desks from left to right. Some people prefer a βουστροφηδόν, serpentine arrangement, taking the first desk from left to right, and the second from right to left. There should, I think, be uniformity in each school, and the arrangement from left to right has in its favour our habits in other things, as in circulating decanters and dealing at whist. Of course, the number seated in each row should be a constant quantity. In counting, the top boy should take the highest number, generally the number of boys on the books of the class, giving the bottom boys the benefit of absentees. Counting downwards saves much trouble in combining the results of occasional examinations with place marks, and the aggregate of the term with the result of the final examination. A great deal may be done by placing questions judiciously. It is a canon of questioning, that attention is best secured by addressing an interrogation to the whole class, before you say who is to answer it. But some sort of order is both fair and convenient. If you wish to give the bottom boys a chance, you will work regularly upwards, with occasional diversions; if you suspect idleness near the top, you will ask the same boy several questions in succession. It has occurred to everyone to pass on questions after they have been answered correctly, particularly where there are only two or three possible answers. You not only shuffle the class, but make boys think instead of guessing. But the best way of shuffling is by written work. A frequent rearrangement by exercises, provided they are done under equal conditions[1], obviously suggests itself. Even in *vivâ voce* lessons, History, for example,—it is a good plan to begin by distributing scraps of paper, and having half-a-dozen questions answered by all. You can look over thirty of them in five minutes, or sometimes trust the boys to mark them themselves. Then, when they are arranged by the result, you are at liberty to proceed with that fire of *teaching* questions which has been compared to the Socratic method, or to the interrogations of a barrister addressed to a witness. I need hardly say that an art of asking such questions is one to be specially cultivated. Sometimes, again, if there is but little change in a lesson, it is desirable not to mark at all, or to put the places down only for the sake of record, as some boys are sure to forget them, and to draw your pen through them so that they do not count in the total. Your lesson may be largely taken up with explanations, and the changes may be insignificant, so that your marks, if added in, would really give double value to the previous lesson. A difficulty often arises as to questions outside the lesson, or questions bringing out general intelligence. Most bright teachers go off at a tangent now and then, and are led by some suggestion to ask a question about the Prime Minister of France, or the contents of the British Museum. It is a good plan, if you think of it, to take a show of hands when such a question is asked, and limit the number of places a boy gains, so as not

---

[1] The difficulty of allowing for assistance given to boys in preparing their "Home-work" is often a serious one. The assistance may be judicious, and ought then not to be discouraged. Like many other problems, *solvitur ambulando*.

to give to general knowledge too large a share of the reward meant mainly for ordinary industry. It is not good for the *moral* of a class if an idle boy is always getting to the top in his Latin lessons by familiarity with English politics or Scott's novels; but it is very good that miscellaneous topics should sometimes be hooked on to the Latin lesson, and that miscellaneous knowledge should receive reasonable encouragement[1].

But there is a limit to the usefulness of place-taking. Very few masters would use it in the highest forms; many would banish it even from the middle forms. It seems, at any rate, to be one of those childish things that should be gradually put away, and ought hardly to continue much above the place where boys begin to be "set on" to construe six or seven lines of an author. It is not easy to find an altogether satisfactory substitute. Written work can, of course, be accurately marked, and to ordinary exercises I should be disposed to add an examination paper about once in three weeks. For daily lessons, the usual plan is to give marks each time a boy is put on to construe, and count the number of questions he answers, either recording them one's self, or letting the boys note them down. Either involves asking questions regularly round—which is not an unmixed good. To let boys keep them for themselves may, in some few cases, open a door to dishonesty; for the master to

---

[1] I owe to Mr Fairbanks of Clifton an ingenious suggestion for diminishing the injustice of place-taking. He would mark only the places gained or lost in each lesson. To avoid negative quantities, each boy is allowed 10 marks a lesson, like the sines and cosines in a table of logarithms. Of course, in this system, when a boy gets to the top, he begins his circuit again, and may make two or three rounds in a lesson. But then he is probably ready for promotion.

record them is a distraction, though not a serious one to anyone who is used to it. It seems, however, to have horrified Dr Wiese, on his last visit to England; and, as it is good to see ourselves as others see us, I will read a few lines from his "Deutsche Briefe über englische Erziehung". "Such a lesson," he says, "which becomes a sort of intellectual communion between the master and his class, is impossible when the teacher is constantly compelled to fix his attention on accessories. But I have reason to think that this is still the case in many English schools. Only imagine! I was present at a Sixth-form lesson, where Thucydides or Tacitus was being read. The master had the author open before him, and his mark-book beside it. His questions were asked only in regular order, and, after each answer, he entered a number opposite the name of the boy who had given it—the number of marks, in fact, which the answer deserved! After the lesson the boys came round his desk to find out how many marks they had got, and entered them in their own memorandum-books. At the end of the week the marks were added up, and the grand total counted in the determination of the final order and the award of prizes. Such a system, even in the highest part of the school, has at least the advantage of compelling the master to pay attention to the whole class, instead of confining himself to a few. But teachers with a higher ideal are undoubtedly embarrassed both by the demands of external examiners, and by the competition for places and prizes." I appreciate Dr Wiese's criticism, but I think I could say something on the other side.

In this connection, the marking of written work, of which I have spoken so fully already, suggests one or two difficult questions. How is the adequate correction of exercises to be effectively carried on without overburdening teachers? Many an hour is spent over dreary routine which would be better employed in reading, or in regaining that freshness and elasticity of spirits without which a schoolmaster is almost useless. On the other hand, it is one of the golden rules of the schoolmaster's art, that any written production should be carefully revised and returned as soon as possible. When to exercises and translations we add notes of science and history lectures, the task becomes a very serious one. The ideal form of correction is, no doubt, the system best known in its application to original copies of verses or Latin essays. The tutor goes through the verses with each boy separately, correcting, criticising, and, as much as possible, following his line of thought, and putting it into a better form. Such criticism is laborious, no doubt, and ill adapted to day schools, where it is hard to get hold of boys out of school hours. But the personal intercourse with boys that it brings about, and the chance of understanding their real difficulties, and of meeting them as you cannot meet them in a general talk, fully compensates for the consumption of time; and no one who has been accustomed to it will drop it without regret. Next, but "longo proximus intervallo", comes the plan of talking to the class in general, after a good deal of red ink or pencilling applied to the individual exercises. If it is possible to add two or three minutes with each boy, to show him his own blunders, this does not fall quite so far short of the first plan. For *exercises*, properly so called, it is adequate. Of course, in both cases, the master *marks* the exercise. There is a third system, supposed to be economical of a master's time, in which the exercises do not pass through the master's hands at all, or only in the most cursory way. The correct version is read out, explained, and perhaps written on the board, while each boy corrects and marks his own or some other boy's exercise. My own experience is strongly against such a system. I have tried it occasionally, but have never been able to work it to my own satisfaction. I believe a few masters succeed with it—

> Pauci, quos aequus amavit
> Jupiter, aut ardens evexit ad aethera virtus,
> Dis geniti, potuere;

but I found, on questioning a friend who I knew liked the plan, that he took the exercises home afterwards, and revised the marking carefully. I should certainly advise no young schoolmaster to try it. For *teaching* purposes only, it *may* work. Even thus used, it presupposes an unusual desire to learn for learning's sake, and takes away the stimulus of the teacher's approval, who cannot pass a judgment on work he scarcely sees. As a means of giving marks, it has everything against it: it wastes the time of the class, it requires that all mistakes should be counted alike—unless, indeed, a very elaborate system be adopted; it opens the way to disputes, and consequent relaxation of discipline; and it leaves the master, unless he is very sharp, in ignorance of many of the mistakes actually made. One is placed in this dilemma:—if only the time really necessary for explanation be given, the marking will be slovenly, and, what is worse, disputed; if full time be given to marking, the energies of the class are wasted on routine which might be performed by the master out of school. I believe one distinguished schoolmaster solved the difficulty by employing some lads who had just left school, and were willing to earn a little money, to put the red-ink lines and reckon the mistakes, leaving the master to explain only. The plan is well worth imitation, if the right lads can be found. One suggestion I would offer, as tending both to save trouble and to increase efficiency—a very rare combination. It is to spare no effort in explaining an exercise beforehand, and, without actually going through it, to make quite sure that every boy knows exactly what he has to do, and how to do it. There *ought* to be no thoroughly bad exercises in a class. No doubt, excessive guidance is not good for boys; it is well, however, to remember that an exercise need not be all *grit;* it is not fair to young boys to accumulate two or three problems in one sentence. There is a great difference between doing something right once with mental effort, and habitually and unconsciously doing it right, and therefore some sameness is allowable. It is worth adding, that rigorously conscientious marking of all written work is in itself the best preventive of having too much to mark. A man who is resolved never to shirk any manuscript becomes unconsciously more careful in seeing that what he does look over is worth the trouble. Instead of notes on a whole lecture, he will have some definite point written out more fully; instead of the next ten sentences in the exercise-book, he will construct an exercise for himself to illustrate what he wants to teach. Some of the best teachers would like every master to make his own exercises; and there is much to be said for it.

I now pass to the last head—the reduction and combination of marks. The first question that arises is that of averages for absence. The marks corresponding to an absence of a few days in a place-taking class are, of course, easily supplied. In the case of longer absences, and a more complicated system of marking, some discretion is wanted, and it is not safe to trust to routine. Suppose, for example, that your marks are made up monthly, and that a boy has been absent during one of three months that make up a term, it would not be right to give him at once the average of the other two. The only case in which it would be right, would be when the marks of the head boy are the same for each of the three months. Take a simple instance, which often occurs. The head boy gets about 400 in each of the first two months, 250 in the third month, which is generally shortened by examinations and the preparation for them. The third boy was present the first two months, obtaining about 360 each month. If you give him an average by the rough method for the third month, his total will be 1080, or 30 ahead of the boy who was head of the class throughout. There is more than one fair way of taking such an average. We might add up the marks of the first few boys for the first two months, and find that our friend is third, but rather nearer to the fourth boy than to the second. We need then only interpolate his marks for the whole term after the second for the whole term, taking care to make him again a little nearer to the fourth. Or if, as often happens, the same boy was head in all three months, the absentee might have his proportion of the head boy's total; that is, in this case, 10 per cent. less, or 945. There are two obvious principles in giving averages—(1) if you are startled by the result of an average, you have certainly taken it wrong; and (2) in doubtful cases, a boy should lose rather than gain by absence—certainly, in no case, gain.

I believe there are persons to whom the *reduction* of marks is a troublesome operation, but it is absolutely necessary where the results of term and examination, or of examinations in several subjects, have to be combined.

It is a very common practice at schools, instead of having absolute maxima, to assume the head boy's marks as the maximum. An absolute maximum, in fact, means very little, except in examinations properly controlled by tradition and mutual checking, like the Cambridge Triposes. In public examinations, at least such as I have had to do with, where each examiner wanders at his own sweet will, the maximum is the most independent variable I ever encountered. But to return, the problem of reduction is, of course, this:—the head boy A. gets 437, B. 362; what is B. to have when A. is reduced to 100? Strictly speaking, a proportion sum is wanted in each case, which requires some labour—very often a little ingenuity will shorten it. In this case, for example, which was selected quite at random, I should deduct 1 per cent., bringing it to 433, which is $4\frac{1}{3}$ hundreds, then deduct $\frac{1}{13}$ bringing it to 400, and lastly divide by 4. So the 362 would become 358, $\frac{1}{13}$ is 28, write down 330, divide by 4 and you have 82. But, modern civilization has saved us even this slight trouble by the instrument I hold in my hand, the Harrow Mark Reducer (to be had of Messrs Aston and Mander), a slide-rule, from which corresponding numbers can be read off at once.

There is a question connected with reduction that often agitates common-rooms and even masters' meetings—Shall the minimum be fixed as well as the maximum? Take this case: Mr A. teaches a class, and marks high throughout, so that, when his marks come to be reduced, they range from 1000 to 600 only; it is examined by Mr B., who is a slashing marker, and brings out his results ranging from 1000 to 200. The range in the one case is 400 marks, in the other 800, so that the examination, instead of telling equally with term marks, counts double. For example, Mr A.'s last boy is half-way up the class in examination; his grand total is 600 + 600, or 1200. Now, he ought, obviously, to be equal to a boy who is half-way up in term, but last in examination, that is, to a boy who gets 800 in term + 200 in examination. You will see that he is 200 marks above him, and that simply owing to the personal equation of the two masters. I know of no means of eliminating personal equation, except that of reducing the marks, so that the top boy has the maximum and the last boy 0. There are strong arguments against such a system, as tending to discourage the lower boys in a class; it requires, too, some correction when one boy is overwhelmingly behind the rest. My own impression is that it is the fairest, but I should be sorry to dogmatize.

I will conclude by working out, if you will allow me, a problem in the combination of marks, of a kind that often occurs where the system of promotion is at all elaborate. I am myself working in a school where the promotion in every subject is independent, and where what little complication there is, is in the distribution of the classes by the head-master. In most schools, a different system is adopted. The forms, properly so-called, are taught together in Classics and English subjects, each group of three or four forms being redistributed for their Mathematics, Modern Languages, and Science, and promotions from *form* to *form* being made by the aggregate of marks from all sources. Let us take a form of 26 boys, the members of which are distributed among 4 mathematical sets, and let us suppose that 200 marks are to be given for mathematics. Now, it is possible to arrange beforehand that the mathematical masters shall send in their marks for each class to a given standard, say the highest set 200, the 2nd 150, the 3rd 100, the 4th 50. The result will be chaos. You have in the form, for example, the head boy of the 2nd set, who gets his 150; the boys of the 1st set, being about the middle of their set, get only 110 or 120. In fact, the marks become *periculosae plenum opus aleae;* they pass entirely out of one's control.

Let us, then, look into the conditions of the problem. Suppose the 26 boys formed an arithmetical progression in respect of mathematical industry and knowledge, we should distribute them along our scale from 200 to 0, at intervals of 7 or 8 marks, thus: 200—192—184—176, and so on. And, in reality, allowing for expansions here and contractions there, such a distribution is what we want to accomplish. If they were to take places day after day, were always to come out in the same order, and to count from 0 to 25, the figures of that scale would correspond to their actual marks. The evenly divided scale is, then, a first approximation to what we want. Now, let us proceed a step further. The best boy in the 2nd set is nearly always, in point of industry, and generally in point of actual performance, superior to the last boy of the 1st set, and so on. Again, the differences among the head boys are more important than those among the lower boys, and require to be accentuated accordingly. But they must not be accentuated so as to swamp the differences lower down. I will suppose there are three boys of the form, A, B, C, in the 1st set; eight, D to K, in the 2nd; eleven, L to V, in the 3rd; and four, W to Z, in the 4th. I should ask all the mathematical masters to send me their marks so that *their* top boy has 200, their last boy 0. Next, I should allot a certain part of the scale to each mathematical set, so that the highest boy in that set could not rise beyond a certain maximum, nor the lowest boy fall below a certain minimum. In the subjoined table the part allotted to the

ON MARKING. 27

3 boys in the first set is 165 to 200, say 17 apiece; that to the 12 boys in the 2nd set, 90 to 175, say 12 apiece; and that to the 3rd and 4th sets, 15 to 105, and 0 to 25, or about 8 apiece. Then we shall have the following results:—

		Actual Marks.	Reduced Marks.
Set I.	A.	117	165 + 35 = 200
	B.	93	165 + 28 = 193
	C.	17	165 + 5 = 170
Set II.	D.	200	90 + 85 = 175
	E.	182	90 + 75 = 165
	F.	127	90 + 54 = 144
	...	...	...
	I.	70	90 + 30 = 120
	J.	29	90 + 13 = 103
	K.	0	90 + 0 = 90
Set III.	L.	185	15 + 83 = 98
	M.	170	15 + 76 = 91
	...	...	...
	U.	40	15 + 18 = 33
	V.	11	15 + 5 = 20
Set IV.	W.	200	25
	X.	154	13
	Y.	117	4
	Z.	100	0

In the lowest set, Z is treated as the worst mathematician of the *form*, and therefore has 0. His marks (100) are subtracted from W, X and Y, whose reduced marks represent their superiority to Z, not to the lowest boy of their own set. In the higher sets, the marks sent in are reduced to a maximum determined as above (35, 85, 90), and added to a fixed minimum (165, 90, 15).

In conclusion, permit me to thank you for the kindness and patience with which you have followed me through so many details. I have tried to put the common-sense view of part of a schoolmaster's routine. But I need hardly remind you that routine and common-sense cover but a small part of what goes to make a good schoolmaster. Beyond all our machinery, the real incentives to study are a keen sense of the value of the teacher's approbation or disapprobation, the sense of duty, and that contagious enthusiasm for learning, which can only be caught from those who possess it; the first strongest in the earliest years of acquirement, the last only developing fully at a later stage. Common-sense and a mastery of routine will generally save us from failure; genuine success in the government of boys can only be attained through those higher qualities that are essential to the government of men.

ON STIMULUS.

By ARTHUR SIDGWICK, M.A.

FELLOW AND TUTOR OF CORPUS CHRISTI COLLEGE, OXFORD,
AND LATE ASSISTANT MASTER AT RUGBY SCHOOL.

ON STIMULUS.

I suppose it is clear that the intention of the Syndicate in instituting this term's course of lectures, one of which I have the honour of being asked to deliver, was to supplement the instruction which they have provided in the theory of teaching by inviting some of those who have had several years of practical experience to contribute what suggestions or guidance that experience may have enabled them to offer. The task which I propose to myself this afternoon, in accordance with this intention, is to say a few words on *stimulus*, viewed from the practical side. Apart from all educational theories, the question which I raise, and to which I shall do my best to find some sort of an answer, is this: to what qualities or methods is due the success which the best teachers achieve in stirring their pupils to attentiveness, to interest in their work, and generally to intellectual keenness and growth. And of these qualities and methods I shall try to direct particular attention to those which are capable of being adopted or acquired, and are not merely matters of natural gift.

I had better state plainly at the outset that my experience, such as it is, is derived from 15 years' teaching at Rugby and three at Oxford; that at school I taught, almost entirely, classics (including composition), history, English, and divinity. Of mathematics and French and German my experience has been limited to an occasional lesson. Of science I know nothing, I have not even taught it. At Oxford I have taught nothing but classics[1]. Moreover, my experience has been almost wholly of boys. Of girls I know nothing, except what I may have got by once examining a girls' school, by a few lessons in Latin and Greek to occasional pupils, by correspondence-teaching in English Literature and composition, and by a course of lectures on English to a girls' college. I thought it better to state this clearly, that it may be plain where I am speaking at first hand, and where I am merely repeating the experience of others.

One great difficulty of my subject, at which I have already hinted, everyone will feel at once. It is this, that the power of stimulating pupils is so largely a matter of natural aptitude, a special form of genius, that it becomes not only very difficult to analyze, but it may even seem that the whole topic is rather out of the beat of a lecture on the practical art of teaching. To dwell on the need of stimulus to one who would be a teacher is like Ruskin's first rule given to the art student, 'Be born with genius'. It is true no doubt that in all branches of teaching the lively and attractive

---

[1] I mention my Oxford experience for the sake of completeness: but the reader will see that it is school-teaching alone which is treated in the lecture. Of teaching Undergraduates I have only the limited experience of three years in my own small but distinguished college. As far as such experience enables me to speak I should be inclined to say that manner is of less importance and matter of more importance than with boys.

manner, quickness and adaptability and resource, insight into character and the orator's instinctive sympathy with his audience, real personal interest both in the studies and the students, force and variety and felicity of expression, wide and accurate knowledge, the power of seizing on the telling points of a subject and presenting them suitably, apt and copious illustration, and above all a strong personality and highmindedness of character—all these are most powerful stimulants to young natures brought under their influence, and all or most of them very hard, if not impossible, to give rules or hints for acquiring. They constitute, or they go far to constitute, the genius of the teacher. But this genius, like others, may be observed in the working; and something may be got by so observing the details of its work. And though few or no teachers possess all these things, all of us have some of them, or the elements of some of them: and something may be done by trying to see what requires cultivation and how it should be attempted. And even those teachers who can lay no claim to the possession of genius may make an enormous difference in their power of stimulating by seeing what to aim at. And further, there are not a few points of detail and method quite capable of being acquired by care and effort, which again may increase immensely the teacher's power of stimulus. I believe, in spite of the difficulty, the subject has its practical side: and on that side I shall try to help you to approach it.

I mentioned just now three things to which the teacher can excite the pupils, attentiveness, interest in their work, and generally intellectual keenness and growth. Of course these three things are often found together, and indeed usually where one is there will be something of the others. But they may be treated separately, and they are often present in very different proportions. One of the most stimulating teachers I have known could not keep a class orderly or attentive at all; he stimulated only the few, but them much. And we most of us have had at one time or another the bad luck to be under a teacher who kept his class perfectly attentive, who yet bored them inexpressibly, and the total result of whose teaching was rather to disgust the pupil with learning—a stimulus of the negative and evil kind. The awakening of attentiveness may thus be regarded apart from other forms of stimulus, as the lowest form of it. Let me begin with a few words about it.

I quite agree with what may be called the commonplace of education, that the first requisite in a teacher is that he shall be able to secure the attention of his class. Those who cannot do this have mistaken their vocation, and whatever other qualities they may have in teaching, to the mass of boys they do more harm than good. They ought not to be teachers at all, and I shall say no more about them. Those who have the power of securing attention can usually do it with ease—at any rate after a short time, when they have learnt their business. The danger for these—a danger I think not sufficiently observed—is that it is too easy. It may be overdone. I do not of course mean that a class can be made too attentive: but they can easily be made attentive by the wrong means and in the wrong way. Learning is hard, and boys are easily bored: and it is natural and right that they should be easily bored. And the teacher should always remember that it is his business, not to make them attend when they are bored, but to make them attend by not boring them. Let me put a very humble instance as a parable. If Jones begins talking to Smith when you are explaining how Cæsar made his bridge, there are three courses open to you. The first is to go on explaining how Cæsar made his bridge, and take no notice of Jones. That is the course of the bad disciplinarian. The second is to say, 'Jones, don't talk'. Here we have the good disciplinarian, as he is called; but the bad teacher. The right way is very likely all the time to go and draw the bridge on the slate, or better still, perhaps, to make Jones or Smith go and draw it, and let Robinson correct him where he blunders, and then go above them both. That is stimulus. I well remember a boy to whom I taught very little, but from whom I learnt one valuable lesson. I had been expounding something, no doubt very wisely and accurately, but without due regard to the different capacities of the top and bottom of the form—a daily mistake of schoolmasters—and when I had done I noticed this boy writing a letter or doing something wholly irrelevant. I rebuked him, and he replied, with what was rather gaucherie than impudence, 'I thought you were only talking'. Schoolmasters—even in the best-regulated forms—are often 'only talking', and 'only talking' is not stimulus.

Of course I do not mean that a teacher will never have to recall his boys' attention by a rebuke in the course of a lesson. He will often have to do so. But I do mean that there is, in what are called well-managed forms, too much of this. When I hear that a man's form is so well in hand that there is never a whisper, I know at once this is overdone. There are two ways of making a form attentive; discipline and stimulus. Those forms where there is never a whisper are governed by discipline alone. Discipline must be always at hand and ready; but stimulus is the more excellent way. A form kept attentive by stimulus is as different as possible to the eye from a form kept attentive by discipline. In the former there is life. In the latter there is stagnation. Schoolmasters, like other despots, sometimes make a wilderness and call it peace. It is tempting because it gives them no trouble. But it is bad. I will illustrate my meaning by an analogy. At Rugby we used to have a lesson before breakfast, seven to eight. It was always the quietest lesson; somnolence and hunger combined made the boys indisposed to any movement. After breakfast they came back different creatures: there was more vitality. There was less of the pin-dropping silence of the morning hour: but for real teaching the second was the best. And some masters act like hunger on the boys: others act like breakfast. To put it in one word: —in a form there should be attentiveness, but there should also be life: attentiveness without life is a mistake.

How then are we to stimulate this attentiveness? The obvious answer is, by making the lessons as interesting and amusing as possible. Interesting of course: but how? First, manner goes for something. The teacher should be as easy and friendly and familiar as he can: all stiffness is a mistake. 'But a schoolmaster must keep up his dignity'. If that means he must not make a buffoon of himself, and must not allow liberties to be taken with him,—then certainly *yes*. But my experience is that what is usually called at school 'keeping up your dignity' is altogether a mistake. My advice to a young teacher would certainly be, think about interesting and amusing your pupils in their lessons, and let your dignity take care of itself. It is not the interesting masters with whom liberties are taken: it is the helpless. You should put no artificial restrictions upon yourself. You should be able to say anything you like or want to say to your form: any illustration, any anecdote or jest which is in point, any perfectly familiar address or appeal, I would even say any digression—in short let the footing on which you are with your boys be natural. The English boy likes to be easy with his teacher: and he perfectly understands the difference between familiarity and impertinence. Familiarity breeds—affection and respect and attention. The least approach to impertinence can be easily stopped by a word, even a look: and if you have a really coarse specimen to deal with—they are getting astonishingly rare in schools since the spirit of the nineteenth century has introduced new relations more friendly and natural between master and boy—but if you do get them, they are quite easy to deal with. The master has the whole situation in his hands: he has the whole power: he can punish if need be. No violence is needed: the quieter you are the better. Send the culprit out of the room and speak to him quietly afterward. Rhetorical reproof and theatric punishments—such as school-tales delight in—are always a mistake. And if you are on friendly relations with your form, an impertinence is a sin against public opinion, and you have the boys with you in quietly disposing of the offender. It may have been observed that I have said 'interesting and *amusing*'. Do I really mean *amusing?* Yes, certainly, as amusing as possible. I don't mean necessarily that the master should make jokes, for the simple reason, if for no other, that jokes are so often not amusing. But he should not be afraid of a joke if it comes his way. For instance, I remember being present when a boy, being read out bottom of a grammar paper, said playfully but respectfully 'I think there must have been some mistake, sir'. To whom the master replied gently 'I think there must have been a good many'. The form were hugely delighted, and for the rest of the hour worked all the better for it. But you may amuse your form, and stimulate them by amusement, in a hundred ways without making jokes. For instance. In a form lesson, particularly with young boys, everything that admits of it should be drawn on the slate, instead of being explained in words, as I said just now of Cæsar's bridge. If you are doing Vergil's plough, you, or better one or two of the boys, should be commissioned to make one of cork and cardboard. Both maker and admirers will be amused, and all will remember *temo, aures, buris, culter*, to their dying day. If you are doing Syracuse in Thucydides, let them make a model of clay, and they will never forget the ground, and will be amused as well. And you can often amuse them and stimulate their flagging attention, where the subject is not so concrete, by taking a little pains. An instance of a construction may sometimes be made rememberable by being amusing instead of dull[1]. Again you may take pains to select your illustrations from a boy's own experience, and so stimulate his attention and memory. A boy is much more likely to listen and remember when you are explaining

---

[1] For example: In Prof. Jebb's excellent edition of Sophocles' *Electra*, there is a note in which he explains the difference between the two Greek expressions ὅρα μὴ τίθης (indicative) and ὅρα μὴ τιθῇς (subjunctive): a rather subtle point of Greek syntax. He illustrates it in the following manner: suppose a man writing at one end of the room: a man at the other end if he suspected the writer of making a mistake, would say ὅρα μὴ ἁμαρτάνῃς (subj.), 'beware lest you *make* a mistake': but if he came and looked over his shoulder and saw the error, he would say ὅρα μὴ ἁμαρτάνεις (ind.), 'beware lest you *are making* a mistake'. This happy and vivid illustration excites the attention and remains as a landmark in the memory, *because it is amusing*. And at Oxford I have had this particular illustration over and over again sent up to me in examination.

the figure *meiosis* if you tell him that his common phrase 'an average long way' is meiosis. Lord Macaulay was stimulating the memory and attention when he gave as an example of the Saturnian metre 'The queen was in the parlour, eating bread and honey.' Mr Bowen, of Harrow, a teacher of rare genius, once preached a striking sermon on public spirit in one sentence, by quietly remarking that anybody would sooner be run out at cricket than run his partner out. Again, though regularity and routine in a form are good, if the attention begins to flag, it is often good to vary the routine. A very slight change in the ordinary system may often wake up boys who are getting dulled with the recurring round. To make them write those parts of the lesson which they usually say, or do *viva voce* what they usually write; to alter the order in which things are done; to stop construing and make them all answer a couple of questions on a bit of paper and then look over each others' work; to set an English poem instead of the ordinary theme; to dart questions at random instead of passing down the line; to let them do a bit of Greek play taking parts, instead of translating one after another—anything for a variety—sometimes even a change of position to relieve the monotony of an hour's sitting, or to send a specially restless boy on a message to the next room—all these and a hundred other such devices are little things, but little things that tend to stimulus in the matter of attention. The teacher's mind and sympathy should be constantly active on the point, and he should cultivate fertility of resource in these little things. 'The nature of man is fond of novelty', says the Eton Grammar: and the nature of boy is a thousand times more so, especially when his quick young limbs are planted on the same square foot of hard board for an hour in a summer morning.

I have tried to suggest in this necessarily brief sketch a few of the true methods of stimulating attention in a common form lesson. There are two false methods on which I should like to say a word: they are what I will call the satirical and the nagging. I will take the nagging first. By nagging I mean a constant fire of little rebukes to one and another for inattentiveness. It wears out the patience of the best-regulated boy to receive or even to hear such rebukes. It is exasperating to human nature, and is utterly futile. Moreover it distracts and worries the teacher, and destroys even what chance there was of any real stimulus to attention. My own advice would be this—you may have in many lessons to caution once or twice; but if you find the thing becoming common, look elsewhere for the cause and for the cure. The probability is you are becoming dull. Either quicken up a bit, or at any rate vary the proceedings. But don't nag. It may of course be not your fault. The weather may be hot: or there may be some excitement toward: a great match after school, or races in the vicinity, or some new promotions to the eleven, or news has come that the ice bears on the reservoir. Any how don't nag. If it is hot, open the door and any remaining window: if it is an excitement, try and compete with it, rather than choke it by nagging. I have learnt the futility of this method by having tried it,—and failed.

The other false method is satire. Whatever a man can or cannot learn, he can at least learn to avoid that. It is nearly always a fatal mistake. Perhaps occasionally, if used among older boys high up, and only very rarely, and only under real provocation, and used in a kindly spirit, and by a man known to the boys to be really kind, and finally to the right boy, it may be successful once in a way as a stimulus. I need scarcely say these conditions are rarely all observed. It tends to become a habit and be used indiscriminately: it reacts on the master's temper: and it is very hard to know the right boy. Many a boy will sit and seem stolid, and all the while resent your satire with exasperation. You cannot tell a sensitive boy by the look. He is not the shy dark-eyed creature of the school tales. He may just as likely be a ruddy high-spirited person, or a brawny athlete, or an ugly lumpy log of a boy. And the satire may often be unjust. And just or unjust, nineteen boys out of twenty hate it. The worst mistake of all is to use it among small boys. They never understand it, and they always think you a brute. And unfortunately it is here that it is commonest. A clever young man comes as an Assistant from the Universities where talk is keen and eager, and satire good or bad is rampant, and he is set down—by the wisdom of headmasters —to teach small boys. When they are ignorant, or inattentive, or stupid, he begins to be sarcastic, i.e. to show a far worse ignorance and stupidity than theirs. They don't know what he means: they think he is hard on them: they are aware that he is laughing at them: they set him down as dull and bitter: and all his good qualities go for nothing. Moreover it feels to them like an abuse of his position. He is older and cleverer than they are, and of course can 'score off' them if he tries, and say clever things at their expense: especially as they cannot reply. They think it unfair: and they are right. I knew a boy who said to a master in a moment of intimacy, 'Oh, sir, I'll tell you a story which will amuse you, *as you are fond of bullying*'. It is difficult to imagine a bitterer thing said by an unconscious boy to an earnest teacher, as he was: and I know that the man felt it deeply.

So far I have been dealing with the lowest form of stimulus, that which can be applied to make boys attentive in school. I must now pass on to the more important kind, the stimulus which stirs them *to love of work, and interest in it*. Of course as the two are closely connected, much of what was said on the last head applies here too. The man who makes his boys attend will also be the man who by the same and allied methods will make them interested in their work. The boys attend because they are interested. That is true; but the question how to make them really interested in their work is a larger question than the other, how to make them attentive in school. It is larger, and it involves other methods and qualities in the teacher; and we have now to ask what these are, and how far they can be acquired by the young educator.

In this part of my subject the detailed points to which I shall have to draw attention differ a good deal according to the nature of the subject that is being taught. I think it will be better first to take construing lessons, understanding that term to mean Latin and Greek construing lessons, and to include repetition and grammar: next to take Latin and Greek prose and verse composition, with a few words about English.

First then, construing lessons: how are we to stimulate boys to love of this work? I may remark at once that there is a great difference between the requirements in the case of young boys between the ages of 12 and 15, and older boys from 16 to 19. It requires very much more care and ability —not of course classical ability, but educational ability, a very different thing—to stimulate little boys properly and teach them well, than it does to do the like for the older. When a young man comes from the University, the chances are he is vastly fitter for teaching the older: though he will have plenty to learn even there. And to know how to deal with little boys requires not merely a special training and aptitude: it also requires you to keep your hand in. Most head-masters having been many years away from young boys, have lapsed into ignorance about them: and he is a wise head-master who knows his own ignorance. The beginnings of language are very dull—the moraine of the mountain of classics, as someone well called them. To put spirit into this part of the work, the *manner* of the teacher is all-important: but that we have dealt with. The next requisite is to have appropriate books. The old theory was, start with delectus, then the easy classics. The best conceivable delectus would be bad: the actual delectuses are infamous beyond description[1]. The easy classics are better of course; but no book B.C. being written for children, none is really suitable. This old theory we have changed. There are some excellent Greek and Latin story-books, with sentences sufficiently simple and matter light and amusing, and above all short: shortness is a great point. Think what the most thrilling narrative of Macaulay would be if read at the rate of 10 lines a lesson, 2 pages a week. In the story-books you can do a tale in one or two bites, and then begin another. Again, there are numerous editions of the classics 'cooked' as it is termed; i.e. the difficulties and dulnesses removed, the main plot or story left, and needful help given.

---

[1] I have seen fragments from Aristophanes, totally unintelligible apart from their context, put down among the earliest Greek sentences for the hapless beginner.

In this most excellent movement I am proud to remember that the first great pioneer was Dr Temple of Rugby. But whatever books there may be, still the greatest care is needed to prevent too hard subjects being chosen for the little boys. Even to understand their difficulties, is a matter requiring the most acute, and laborious, and experienced mind. And the teacher naturally wants to get his boys on. I know by bitter experience of myself and my colleagues that time after time even experienced schoolmasters will make the fatal error of setting the lower forms to read too hard work. Let all teachers be solemnly warned of this.

The next important requisite may seem too obvious to mention: that the teacher should be master of his subject. Or speaking more precisely, I should say that for upper and older boys, in classics, one of the most efficient ways to excite the love of learning, is for the teacher to be himself an eager student. If he does not work hard and read, he will get stale: and staleness is a blight which spreads from mind to mind most rapidly: it will render sound learning unattractive with marvellous rapidity. Of course if his interest in the study reaches the point of enthusiasm, it is the most potent stimulus by far in the world. I was myself under a teacher for a year and a half who was totally inefficient in every other way, but had an absorbing enthusiasm for Greek and Latin scholarship. His tones and his glances as he paused over a fine point of grammar, or a felicitous translation, remain with me to this day. He made us *feel*, without ever saying it, that accurate scholarship was *the* enticing and important study. He had many weaknesses. He kept no order or discipline, he let much go by default, he never accommodated himself to the weaker vessels: and so he influenced only the few: but those he influenced profoundly.

The influence was many-sided. He gave us an ideal; we believed in his knowledge and judgment and taste; he enlarged our horizon: our best efforts were appreciated, and when successful gave him a real personal delight: the failure of our slipshod work was manifest to ourselves. And he sowed his own love of the study in our hearts. Of course such enthusiasm is rare: it is genius. But failing that, eager study, hard work, is most important; and this is in the power of all. For one thing boys are very imitative: and what the teacher cares for, the boys tend to care for too. Again, the mere fact that he is thorough, and takes trouble for them, and is thinking, and doing his best, is borne in upon them sooner or later, and is sure to be a stimulus. An idle man, however clever, in the long run demoralises his form. Again, an unprepared lesson is a dull lesson. The teacher is living from hand to mouth, making out as he goes on: he has not thought out his illustrations, put his expositions into shape, made certain of his decisions on knotty points, &c. He ought to know exactly what he is going to do when he gets into school: or else he is teaching at half steam-power. The holding in hand a class of boys is always a tax on the nervous-system: the brain should have its way clear and be free to act. I spoke at first of its being necessary for *upper boys* that the teacher should work: it will be seen that these latter remarks apply equally to the teacher of lower boys. It is not of course necessary that 10 lines of Xenophon should be prepared like 100 lines of Agamemnon. But in the Xenophon too preparation is required in the way indicated. Nor do I mean that it is at all equally necessary for the teacher of small boys to be a student. Manner, tact, insight, many things of course come before learning for the teacher of small boys. Nay, one may go further than this, and admit that there is a peculiar sort of clever superficial man, who has ideas and picks up things, but knows none thoroughly, who may be even an extremely successful teacher of small boys. They are not deep enough themselves to get to the bottom of him, though the bottom of him may be not far off. And if he is kindhearted and genial he may do very well with them. But let the head-master forbear to put him to any high work. And note that he succeeds by his merits, not by his defects. Ceteris paribus, give me the thorough man. My emphatic advice to the young teacher would be, On no account relax your intellectual efforts or lower your intellectual ideal because you are going to teach boys. Be a student all you can. For the elder boys it is vitally important: on the younger it will not be wasted. To all it is a stimulus.

As to what may be called the accessories of a construing lesson, pictures, drawings, casts, photographs, models, plans, maps, antiquities, &c., in illustration of our texts, the more the better. We have made an immense advance in this matter in recent years: and I have no doubt that very much more advance will be made yet. The classics may be treated as language, as literature, or as part of the ancient life. The language as such appeals to few, if indeed it does appeal to few. The literature appeals to more, but still few, as British human nature goes. The life appeals to many. If we would treat our construing lessons,—without neglecting grammar, and close rendering, and the needful,—with constant reference to the ancient life of which they were a fragment and a record, the stimulus would be far greater. This was attempted by Arnold and Lee, though from lack of materials it went but a little way. Recently museums and lectures at schools have done something, and the most forward of the assistant masters have done more. When a new generation of masters arises themselves trained under the new influences, we may expect a great advance. Meanwhile it is interesting to note, that the first systematic attempt in English to illustrate ancient literature by ancient art has come from a Newnham student[1]. If we help the ladies, they will perhaps return the favour unexpectedly. I will not dwell farther on this branch of the subject, for I belong I fear to the old school, and the little I have tried of this form of stimulus has been of an ignorant and intermittent kind. But the young are right, and it must be left to them, and we must welcome and applaud their better methods.

The bulk however of a classical lesson must still consist of language: construing, analysis, grammar. What is the most stimulating way of dealing with these? There are numerous difficulties small and great; one is, that in all schools, and especially in small schools, the forms are so unequal. If you teach the top, you are over the head of the bottom; if you let the bottom boggle through the lesson, you are boring the top. Every teacher will feel this difficulty: he must meet it by tact and compromise: turn and turn about; easy things to the stupid, a little teaching directed to each order of mind in every lesson, and so forth. As to the actual translation, the real way, it seems

---

[1] *Myths of the Odyssey in Art and Literature*, by J. E. Harrison. Rivingtons, 1882. The book is a most interesting and attractive one: and its genuine merit and value has been amply attested by far better judges than myself. Miss Harrison was one of the first Newnham students who read for classical honours at Cambridge.

It should not be forgotten that Mr Oscar Browning was the first to draw public attention in a practical way to the need of using the study of art and archæology to illustrate classical form teaching, in a paper published some years ago in the *Fortnightly Review*.

to me, to stimulate, is to set a high standard, to prepare carefully yourself, but to accept thankfully from boys anything that shews search or effort in the way of idiom, force, or taste. Word-hunting is often an amusement, and good if well kept in hand and each suggestion criticised. The boys should be led up to a good translation if possible, by the developing process; all contributing. Notes in school-editions are often dreadful offenders in telling too much. If the note gives the rendering cut and dried, there is an end to effort, i.e. to stimulus. At the end of the lesson the master should translate fluently, and give it out well as though he were acting (if a play), speaking (if an orator), reciting (if an epic), &c. The boys get their author delivered in the proper form and continuously, to minds thoroughly awake to the detailed points, and in a style which is wholly beyond their power of producing. The better the master reads, the more stimulating is the process. To this day I remember the effectiveness of Mr Thomas Evans' Sophocles translations, when the lesson was over: and many a Shrewsbury boy would doubtless echo the following words written by a pupil of the great Dr Kennedy. 'He is not merely translating Demosthenes—he *is* Demosthenes speaking extempore in English. The voice is modulated in a most expressive manner—description, question, dilemma, invective, sarcasm —all are rendered in their most appropriate tones. The voice gets louder and the pace quickens as he nears the end, and when he stops, you might hear a pin drop.' That is stimulus in translation.

A word finally about repetition and grammar. Is there any way by which stimulus may be imparted by, to, or along with these 'names of weariness'? Briefly and frankly, if Eton and Winchester will forgive, I do not believe in Latin and Greek repetition, *as a form lesson*, at all. It is supposed to train the memory, to cultivate the taste, to store the mind with models of poetic form and metre, and noble climax!—to prevent false quantities! It may train the memory a little, but it does not do the other things. The only stimulus supplied by repetition, is that which comes to their ear and poetic sense when boys *like* repeating. Most boys like, or would like if properly handled, *English poetry*. The rhyme, the simple metre, and the familiar language, make all the difference. It pleases them, it increases their vocabulary, their ideas, their sense of rhythm and form; sometimes even when quite infants it excites them to write rhymes. In short, it stimulates them. With Latin and Greek verses it is not so. Who ever heard of a boy being stimulated by his repetition to do verses for himself? Nothing can make a repetition-lesson other than dull and mechanical; and I am convinced that in nine cases out of ten it cultivates nothing but the memory, and that with unsuitable material; and is a task generally disliked, involving a heavy and very unequal expense of labour, and is a waste of everybody's time. What I should like to see in schools, and what would be really stimulating to the literary sense, would be to make English poetry the staple subject for repetition, and set long pieces (as extras from time to time) of Latin and Greek poetry to the promising scholars.

With grammar of course it is different. Accidence must be learnt if the boys are to learn the languages systematically at all. The learning must always be a drudgery; it must always seem to the learner a mass of arbitrary irregularities. The mastering of these is not merely a burden: it is even in itself depraving to the mind, initiating it early into a disbelief in law and order. We should recognise that this is a real evil, only borne for the sake of greatly preponderating benefits, and unless these benefits are realized, intolerable. What the stimulating teacher can do is only to lighten the burden. First, in Greek; the new method of consonant and vowel declensions, and the teaching of verbs and nouns by stems, are great improvements, reducing chaos to something like order. Secondly, let the beginner, where examinations allow, learn as little as may be of the out-of-the-way irregular words. Let him avoid primer-doggrels, and needless genders[1]. Thirdly, the accidence should be ingrained, not by mere said lessons of grammar, but by the natural and stimulating method of constant exercise in making easy sentences. Fourthly, don't let the beginner spend too much time on the mere committing of grammar to memory. As soon as ever he knows one declension he should practise it by translating and composing. Translating and composing, i.e. reading and writing one's new language, are stimulating: saying accidence is not. In early teaching there is always too much accidence. With syntax again there is a good way and a bad way, a stimulating and a discouraging way. The rules should be taught as much as possible in the course of reading, then illustrated by writing: and as little as possible by heart. Let the boy have the facts first, then arrange and explain them. I would even go so far as to say, let much of the grammar

---

[1] What can be the use of a lower-school boy learning that *cunae* and *magalia* are only used in the plural: that *colus, pampinus* and *sapphirus* are feminine: that *vespertilio* and *pugio* are masculine, as well as *mugil, ren* and *attagen?* The Public School Primer contains 110 lines on gender and noun anomalies, and about as many on quantity: altogether making a poem as long as Lycidas. I suppose somebody learns them: at any rate they must have been written to be learnt.

wait. Explanations of syntax are dreadfully often given prematurely. And as in the early stages, so in the later, let the teacher carefully recognise the limitations of human faculty. There are many boys who can thoroughly appreciate a Greek play who never for the life of them could discriminate the various uses of the optative. Hundreds of boys can fairly understand and thoroughly enjoy Homer, for ten who can parse him without fault. I am not recommending slip-shod work. I am recommending the observance of a due proportion in the different departments of language-teaching. If the boys parsed every word in ten lines and then read 40 lines, swiftly, and even inaccurately, they would have a far more stimulating and instructive lesson than if they parsed twenty lines thoroughly: and it would be done in less time. They would learn more Greek, and more of other things too. The negative rule then is to teach Syntax principles neither too much nor too soon. The positive rule is mainly this: give them clearly. Choose your instances as striking as you can: use the slate[1] always: write down the sentence, leading on the boys from point to point, with questions and illustrations on the way, contributions if possible from several, keeping their attention awake, till the whole thing is plain before them. If you are discriminating between two different usages or expressions, show the difference by writing out two clauses differing

---

[1] May I put in a word in favour of using a large slate, instead of that odious invention, the painted black board? The slate is easier to write on, clearer to read from, is wiped absolutely clean in an instant, and lasts for ever. The black board is worse both for writing and reading, and is much more easily scratched. It is like a palimpest manuscript; the ghosts of dead instructions are never wholly obliterated from it.

only in the one particular point. Draw their attention to all illustrations of your rule which are to be found in the lesson, and bring it in as soon as you can in their composition. By methods like these you will make your grammar-teaching, I do not say stimulating, but as little depressing as may be.

But it is in composition that stimulus is most important. In other lessons it is the greatest of aids: in composition it is almost the whole matter. I shall treat chiefly of prose, because I see that Dr Abbott, a born teacher of the first rank, is announced to give a lecture in this course on Verses: and from him you will learn, if from any man in England, the true stimulating method of teaching verse-composition. I think then, as I said before, that Prose-composition should begin at once, at the very earliest stage. Not merely is it the best way of practising accidence, but the boy gets from the first the strong stimulus of feeling that he has *produced* something. It is far easier to get a boy to take a pride in his written work than in book-lessons: even careless boys will often become comparatively careful when they have to write. The written work, he knows, will all be seen: it is all his own, with his name at the top: if he is timid or unready (as most boys are) he still has his chance here to do well—many motives combine to make him try his best on paper. This being so, we have scope for stimulus supplied by the very nature of the work and the boy: and it is obviously important to make the most of the opportunity. The first thing, as in construing, is to have the work well within his power. Of course it is true that difficulties are required to nerve the learner to effort: and that to go on at the lower when one can do the higher tends to contempt and carelessness. But the teacher will not make this mistake: he will make the other. The desire to get his pupils on: the constant tendency to over-estimate their powers—(all teachers complain of the stupidity of their boys, which only means they are stupider than the teacher thought, i.e. the teacher is always mistaken and always discovering his mistake and always making it again)—above all the extraordinary difficulty of seeing exactly what will be difficult—these causes will amply protect the teacher against setting too easy composition. At starting, at any rate, the boy should be able to do his exercises perfectly if he gives his whole mind to it. It gives him self-respect and a high standard of work, which once established, he does not like to lower: and this is a powerful stimulus.

The next thing is to make your earliest exercises lively. I preach again the doctrine which I have preached many a time, that even the earliest exercise books should be all stories. If a man takes trouble, he can write his stories in the simplest of clauses, each containing one simple proposition. And a boy likes doing a story better than disconnected sentences. I open the latest exercise book, and I find. 'The poet's pride was not honouring the steward's 'gifts'...'the peltasts in the village had clashed the iron 'arms...the tears of the bride were the beginning of the 'revolt... &c.' What conceivable interest is there in this? It is just as easy to write 'One of the slaves stole the gold. 'The master assembled them all and spoke :—The thief has 'a feather in his nose. The others remained quiet: but 'the thief plucked his nose. Thus he was discovered and 'received blows'. The boys learn as much Latin or Greek, and they like doing the old Hindoo tale, even if they have heard it before.

When they get a little further, it is a great stimulus to

begin original exercises. It does not do to set original exercises only, because the boy is never made to grapple with definite difficulties. But pari passu with translation-pieces original exercises call out his power. I would still have stories. Let the master tell the boys at the end of the lesson a story viva voce, to be reproduced after their own fashion next morning in Latin. When the boy sits down to do it, the story arises in his mind in its natural English dress, too idiomatic and too complex (though doubtless simple enough), in short too hard, to go straight into Latin. In his own interest he simplifies: and the straits to which he is put, and the effort, and the comparison of tongues involved, and the ingenuity developed—all are a valuable exercise both in thought and in language. It is precisely the process we employ when we begin to talk French or German, and is a most stimulating and instructive one. By and bye he reaches a second stage, when he begins to get some mastery over structure. He appropriates certain constructions or idiomatic turns, and reproduces them in exercise after exercise. This is capital: you praise him: he blushes responsive, and gives you a new one next time. When that happens, he is a made man, and will go from strength to strength. And the command and confidence gained in the original exercise will help him in the set translation piece, where he cannot shirk or outwit difficulties but has to face them. I have seen what I am describing: it is no imaginary picture.

The second stage passed, when accidence and ordinary syntax are fairly mastered, we come to the third stage of prose composition, the stage from fifth form onwards, where though syntax has constantly to be studied and maintained, the chief points are idiom and style. This is the real crux both for teacher and taught. It is the point at which a far larger number break down than anywhere else. And nowhere else is stimulus so needful and so difficult. Accidence can be mastered by judicious drilling. Syntax can be fairly mastered by any boy not a real dolt (and there are very few), if he be properly taught and properly willing to learn. But style requires some elements at least of the literary sense. A boy may look at the Latin, work at it, read it, translate it, try to imitate it, perfectly understand it, and yet all the while miss the style. The question is, how to help him to see it? The subject is very wide, and I cannot do more than indicate a few of the leading points. First, to set good pieces, and let the pupil have good models in his authors. If it be speech or description, let it be stirring; if narrative or essay, let it be pleasant and amusing. A good piece in the English, I have noticed time after time, produces good exercises, where a duller though easier piece would have been worse done. And it is obviously wise to do pieces more or less like the authors being read. If no author is being read—and one cannot always be doing Latin Prose—it is not a bad plan to have a small selection of well-known Latin bits—like Walford's Cicero, an excellent book—to which to refer the boys, and urge them to read one or two before setting to work. Secondly, we can narrow the ground by instilling two or three main principles, with *constant* and *copious* and *telling* illustrations: such for example as the principle of turning English *abstracts* into classical concretes; the principle of turning English *metaphors* into plain statement; the principle of *connection* of clauses; the principle of *order to gain clearness*; the principle of making in Latin and Greek *the people do the things* where in English we employ phrases like 'silence reigned', 'misgivings seized him', 'the retrospect was glowing', 'the news was far from removing their suspicions', &c.; the principle, finally, of interpreting into clear sense what in English is hinted, inferred, alluded to. Thirdly, let us be keen to detect, amid mountains of crudeness and awkwardness, the germs of thought, of effort, of grappling with the difficulties. The boys will fail again and again after they have begun to try: it is vital to give them prompt and generous encouragement. Fourthly, the good and stimulating composition teacher will make effective play in construing lessons; he will often stop sharply and shew the boys when they have with ease or difficulty got the right English idiom for the Latin, that there before their eyes is the way to do it back again. The boy is thinking of the hard journey from classics to English; he is not thinking of the return journey: but a word will make him think. And what shall I say finally of model versions by the master, or what are called fair copies? The common plan is, or was, to write them (and let the boys copy), or dictate, or in these hectographic days to multiply and distribute. I am convinced this is no use at all to the boys, or at least to the mass. They don't all read them: when they do they rarely understand why or where they are better than their own: for teaching, the fair copy as such is useless. To the master it is absolutely necessary to do the piece as well as he can himself: or else he does not really know the difficulties and cannot properly or promptly correct the copies. But if it is to be of use to the boys, the man should assemble the form, when all the papers are corrected and returned, distribute the fair copies, and then go through it carefully; he should shew exactly where the English is obscure, or idiomatic, or requires rearranging: why he has cut this metaphor, inserted that particle, altered the order, connected in such a way, expanded or modified in such another. In short, he should do the piece before them, reproducing and solving all his own and most of their difficulties. And inasmuch as it often happens that the thing can be done in a great many different ways, he should shew the boys, or better, lead them on to contribute, alternative renderings. Of these alternatives, all possible, some will emerge better than others for sound, or neatness, or effectiveness: and here we have the elements of literary taste. The more copious and quick the teacher is here, the more stimulating.

Into the details of verse-teaching I will not enter, for reasons given above. I will confine myself to four remarks. First, if a boy is not idle and hates his verses, they are wasting his time, and he should do something else. Secondly, in verses, even more emphatically than in prose, I say the way to stimulate is to set good poetry—as soon as the boy can do poetry at all. Some men, in their desire to find what is easy, go on setting trivial and commonplace pieces about birds, and spring, and water, and hearts, and violets. The commonplace English produces necessarily the dull and bald Latin. The pieces should be rich and fresh and striking, with plenty of matter, or what the boys call *sense*, in it. The most plaintive of all laments, 'I cannot do my verses because I have got no sense,' should be ever in the master's mind. Thirdly, for the same reason, if you set the boys original verses, suggest two or three lines of treatment—don't let them make bricks without straw. Fourthly, Greek verses are far easier than Latin.

On English composition I must be content with a few bare suggestions: and here I should say that my experience has been very slight and has been almost confined to girls.

I am convinced, however, from what I have seen that for older pupils, such as these girls were, and I will add with equal confidence, for all, the really stimulating method is the exact opposite of the old system of Themes. That was to teach a certain cut-and-dried method of treatment of all subjects: introduction, reasons, similes, illustration, quotation, conclusion. The real aim of English essays is not so much to teach the pupil to write—still less of course to write in such a deadly and artificial way—as to teach them to read and think. Let them learn no scheme of treatment, aim at no style, but just try to think out the question and write sense: they will soon find, that the best way to get style is to have things to say. Their repetitions and confusions and baldnesses come, as you will easily shew them, not from having no style, but from not having thought their points out: and you will help them to do that by a few questions and hints. You will be careful, particularly if you teach girls, to allow no fine writing and no sermonizing; boys try fine writing, but they do not sermonize. The subjects must of course, as before, be chosen with great care, being such as they are likely to have some knowledge or thoughts about already. It is often good to give a choice of subjects, as is done in examinations. The skilful teacher will weave in questions of the day, questions that arise in their daily life, questions alluded to in the course of the current lessons, or illustrated by them. And perfect freedom should be allowed in the handling; and special praise be given to the least originality of thought or treatment. And, above all, there should be no dogmatism on the teacher's part, no pattern essay or scheme of treatment given as final: the essays should be regarded as each a different search after truth, and the line taken by each writer followed, corrected, enlarged, enriched, made as far as possible consistent, and clear, and cogent.

But I fear I have dwelt too long on the detailed work of a teacher and the stimulus to love of work in the various departments and subdivisions of classical learning. I must hasten to conclude by a few words on the third and highest form of stimulus, namely the methods and qualities by which the teacher can excite the pupil to *general intellectual interest, activity, and growth.*

For making boys think, as opposed to merely cramming them, though there may be higher qualities, there are few more important than clearness. It may seem at first sight as if it was easy to be clear in teaching: in fact there are few things that want more constant attention, and even preparation. To make his own words precise and clear-cut: to put complicated things in lucid order and simple language: to search out for the point, and emphasize that duly; to avoid formulæ as much as may be, and constantly to formulate afresh when the boys begin to use words by rote: when there are difficulties, to shew exactly where the difficulties are: to lead on confused answers till the confusion, and the exact point of the confusion, becomes apparent: to cross-question neatly and succinctly half-knowledge, so as at once to expose its incompleteness and supply the deficiency: to divine exactly in a muddled head what is the particular tangle which has caused the muddle:—these are some of the marks of the really clear teacher, and such clearness is excessively stimulating. Iron sharpeneth iron, and edge produces edge. Nothing is so delightful to the growing mind as to have one after another in an hour's lesson all the cobwebs swept from his mind, till every detail is clearly and fully seized. Dr Bradley, now Dean of Westminster, was remarkable for this precision and incisiveness in teaching: so was Professor Bonamy Price: so was Dr Temple. Closely allied to clearness, also peculiarly exemplified in Dr Temple, comes what I will call grasp: the power of presenting a complex whole so that the youthful mind can seize it. 'Dr Temple would take a chapter of Guizot (I quote the words of one of his best pupils) 'or De Tocqueville, or a book of Livy, or the *Philebus* of Plato, and threw it out on the dissecting table with its skeleton arrangement quite clear, till we marvelled that we had found any difficulty.' I can add my own testimony to this. I remember to this day his lessons on the Epistle to the Romans—the revelation which they were to me in the matter of thought and handling. Everything fell into its place: the fragments became a whole: the maze was mapped. Such clearness and grasp gives the young mind a sense of power and conquest: it makes deep thought and serious argument interesting as such: it disposes to new efforts: it widens, matures, stimulates. And observe that without such grasp and lucidity of exposition we should not merely have gained less from such work: we should have gained nothing at all. Many of the subjects I have mentioned were for the most part out of our reach without it: we should have else been doing work beyond us, with all the consequent confusion, helplessness and discouragement, on which I have before dwelt.

And speaking of this leads me to give one caution, of a danger to which all teachers are exposed, and certainly not least those who are keen and eager, and feel this power of lucid exposition within them. And that is the danger of explaining too much and too soon. It is so tempting, when the boys are all in a muddle, and the subject admits of clear exposition within their power of apprehending, to have recourse at once to the slate and put it all out before them. The danger is lest the boys finding such aid always at hand should relax their own efforts in the face of difficulties and come to rely too much on the teacher. In unseen translations and compositions, where the master does not intervene till the work is done and written out, the boys always have the stimulus of having to meet, and solve as best they can, their own perplexities. In oral lessons the preparation is always more indefinite, and the boy knows he can always say 'I couldn't make it out'. The teacher's business is to judge in each case whether he ought to have been able, and if so, to use a wise reticence: to give a hint, or no help at all, and make him try again. The boys should be made to feel that their powers are gauged, and the master's expectation should be pitched high. To leave a point uncleared up is always a self-denial, especially to a keen and able expounder. But it is a self-denial that is often required, in the true interests of stimulus.

Another potent stimulus to thought and interest is supplied, by getting the pupils, wherever it is possible, in however humble a department of knowledge, to share in anything like original research. It is of course very rarely that boys with their undeveloped powers and narrow knowledge can find work of this kind in a field so thoroughly explored as classics. Some faint approach to it, but not to be despised, may be sometimes found: the boy may be set to find instances of a point of style or grammar for himself: or if there is a mistake in his notes he may be made to correct it: or still more delightful, he may confute his master. I do not say the teacher should make mistakes deliberately for this end: but if he do err and the boy can detect him, the man will welcome this lucky incident for the powerful spur it gives to the boy. But it is in science-work that the chance most often occurs of getting something like real investigation. And here I will say a word of the powerful incitement to thought and interest given by these excellent new school institutions, the Natural History Societies. The whole of the work is voluntary, and the boys take the keenest interest in it. At Rugby we had two really stimulating teachers of a high order, both science masters[1], and they produced in this Natural History Department most valuable results. Several of the other masters also devoted a good deal of time and trouble to the society. The boys worked the district thoroughly in Botany, and very fairly in Entomology. The addition of a new species was an honour much coveted. In Geology similar results were obtained; a large local collection of fossils, and thorough examination of the country. The Society also kept the statistics of the weather: rain and temperature were duly recorded, the boys using all the gauges and instruments. The whole neighbourhood was surveyed by the boys with aneroids, and the survey perpetuated in a clay model. Even the actual scientific results were not absolutely nil. One observer contributed facts for Wallace and one even for Darwin: and one continued an investigation up to the satisfactory end of a paper before the Royal Society. But the recognition, though prized, was the least part of the results. The work was invaluable as a stimulus: it made the boys keen, and careful, and quick, and moved them to aspire to knowledge as to an attractive thing.

---

[1] Mr F. E. Kitchener, now Headmaster of the Newcastle Grammar school: and the Rev. J. M. Wilson, Headmaster of Clifton College.

And this naturally leads us to the last and highest form of mental stimulus, the teacher's own enthusiasm and personal force of character. It is powerful in school lessons, as I have said above, and it is infinitely more powerful in its general influence on the boy's mind: its effect is visible on his whole life and being. Whether it be school lesson or subject of common talk out of school, the enthusiast drags the boy's mind captive. He makes him attend, he makes him interested, he makes him think: without trying to do so he makes learning seem attractive and delightful. Boys are naturally impressionable, and enthusiasm impresses: they are naturally imitative, as I said before, and whatever they see a man keen about, they at once begin to excite themselves about it too. And *all* such enthusiasms are valuable. Whether it be poetry, history, politics, art, science, natural history, or archaeology, the enthusiast will at once make a school of his own imitators about him. And he will do far more than this. He will lift boy after boy out of the barbarous intellectual atmosphere in which the natural boy lives and moves, and make him conscious—though it be only dimly conscious—of the vast world of interest which lies around in every direction, waiting till he gird up his mental loins and come to explore. This is the real result of a master's enthusiasm; it cultivates. Under plodding hum-drum teachers who will not put soul into their work, a boy may pass through a school from bottom to top, doing all the work so as to pass muster, and be a savage at the end. But let the enthusiast catch him, though but for a term, and the savage is converted. I need not cast about for instances: all school-histories *consist* of them. Dr Arnold when he was composing sermons, histories, notes on Thucydides, and teaching Rugby better than any school was ever taught before, was writing letters, as his life shews, on every mortal subject of interest,—the Newmanites, Niebuhr, Rome, the Jews, the Chartists, London University, the French Revolution. This width of interest took hold of the boys as it always does and must. And he himself knew it and felt it. 'The more active my own mind is,' he said, 'the more 'it works upon great moral and political points, the better for 'the school.' With Dr Temple it was the same. His eager interest and his wide knowledge when he talked to us of history, or politics, or literature, or the men of the day, or his Oxford memories, woke up the dullest of us and made us keen to know more. It was the same with Dr Lee of Birmingham, a man who made an extraordinary mark on what was before his time an unimportant school. It was the same with Dr Bradley of Marlborough who taught the fifth at Rugby when I was in it. It was the same with Dr Kennedy of Shrewsbury, as I learn from many friends who were his pupils. Widely different as these men were in many ways, with one and all the boys felt the honour and the delight of contact with large knowledge, and eager interest, and strenuous energy. And they knew that their teacher was always giving them of their best. These of course are the born teachers, who must ever be few. But there are many lesser men, well known in their profession, and some not far behind those greater ones, who have their share of the same qualities, and whose value to their schools is quite beyond estimate. And something of their success I doubt not all can achieve, who will follow in their steps and put their heart into the work.

Lastly, of the greatest stimulus of all in education, the *moral* stimulus, I have not spoken, and I have neither the time nor the intention to speak. Assuredly it is not because

I fail to recognise its primary power and importance. What it was, to come for months or years into daily contact, at the most impressionable time of life, with a man whose every look and tone and word spoke to us of high aims and resolute endeavour, whose life in the sight of the dullest and weakest of us was plainly based on duty and self-devotion, whom all could absolutely trust, to whom the most timid would naturally turn in trouble or perplexity, whom all could love and venerate without reserve—such an experience it is not likely that one who had ever known it could forget or ignore. And to the power of such an influence those who knew it best are least disposed to set a limit. Among boys, even more than among men, it is the one power that transfigures: it gathers grapes of thorns and figs of thistles. But to treat of it lay outside my purpose: and with this one word I leave it.

And one word more I would fain say, if I might without presumption, a word of earnest encouragement to those who mean to make teaching their profession. It is a work, you will be truly told, of hard and constant labour, and much drudgery. But the interest and the delight of it are such as far outweigh the labour. The mere daily life among the young is to the true teacher a constant happiness. And if one have any fitness for the work, and give his heart to it, there is no work so richly rewarded. The gratitude of the young to those who have done their best for them is more fervent and more durable than any other. To any teacher who is near to knowing his own faults and short-comings, such gratitude must always seem far and away beyond his deserts. It is filled full, and pressed down, and running over. And it lasts to the end of life.

A. SIDGWICK.

17 *May* 1882. CAMBRIDGE.

ON THE TEACHING OF LATIN VERSE COMPOSITION.

By E. A. ABBOTT, D.D.
HEAD MASTER OF THE CITY OF LONDON SCHOOL.

ON THE TEACHING OF LATIN VERSE COMPOSITION.

It is very doubtful whether Latin Verse Composition will be, and still more doubtful whether it ought to be, taught in our Public Schools at all a generation hence. But as the wave of the reforming spirit, which passed over the Head-masters of schools some ten years ago, seems for the present to have exhausted its strength, it is possible that Latin Verse-making will not pass away from among us till the end of the present century. I have accordingly selected the subject for this lecture because, as at present taught, it is one of the most tedious, mechanical, and profitless of our school studies, and a teacher's attention may well be drawn to the best means of diminishing the evils, and increasing the benefits, that may result from it.

A few words may suffice as to the present system. Boys generally begin the study young, sometimes as early as 10 or 11, and very often before they have any very clear notions of the difference between poetry and prose. Having mastered the rules of prosody, and learned how to construct tags for the beginning and end of a hexameter or pentameter, they then pass to some Clavis, or Nuces, or Elementa, or other manual, in which they are presented with a mass of words, neither Latin nor English, but a mongrel Latin-English, to be rendered literally into Latin Verse. Seldom attaining any amusing height of absurdity, these exercises generally keep a low level of uncouth obscurity, which is, to say the least, not calculated to train the young reader to appreciate a good English style. Take the following extract from a book of merit above the average. The subject is " Marius ".

"Of him the Libyan shore sees the first triumphs,
  Where, Metellus, thou grievest for war's prizes snatched away,
The great prizes which Jugurtha gave his conqueror, (when) forced
  To go before his triumphal wheels.
Then, as consul, he moves new wars, and conquers and routs
  Alike the bands of the Cimbri and the Teutonic bands."

To make this stuff readily intelligible, some knowledge of the Latin idioms, latent under the English, is almost needful even for older readers; and for younger boys the difficulty of grasping the exact meaning of what they have to translate, is often very great. Naturally, many of them make no attempt to understand it, but, with the aid of their vocabulary, render the lines into Latin word for word, arranging their results like pieces of a puzzle, so as to fit into the metre. I have heard it said, by way of apology for such exercises, that they involve no strain on the young pupils, while they give boys an encouraging sense of the power to accomplish something. But the sense of power thus bestowed is a mere illusion; and surely an exercise is not sufficiently defended on the plea of "involving no strain", if it destroys the appreciation of English idiom and English rhythm, and tends to suppress thought. Indeed, for a boy of any taste and spirit, few tasks of drudgery can be more irritating than to slave for an hour at thirty or forty of these mechanical lines, and to find that a quarter of the time, perhaps, has been spent fruitlessly over a single line, because he has forgotten to avail himself of some particular and probably rare word, which alone can fit into the line, wasting twenty minutes, may-be, in trying to make "bellum" do service in a line which absolutely requires "duellum".

The wastefulness and barrenness of this study in its initial stages are all the more serious because a large number of the pupils will probably drop it before they have attained any power of writing passable Latin verse; so that, for them, the only possible utility lies in some indirect benefits resulting from the work in its elementary stages. For these boys, if there are no such benefits, the subject will have been pure loss; or, in other words, two or three hours a week, of the hours devoted to study from the age of 10 or 11, to the age of 16 or 17, will have been absolutely thrown away.

Without further preface, I will now suggest a new method of teaching Latin Verse Composition, which shall have the following advantages: 1st, by delaying the commencement of the study till the age of 13 or 14, it shall effect a great saving of time; 2nd, it shall begin with a preliminary series of reasonable, interesting, and stimulative lessons, profitable to all alike, whether they continue or discontinue Verse-making; 3rd, this course shall not occupy more (rather less than more) than one hour a week, with a minimum of half an hour of home-work; 4th, by enabling the teacher to distinguish rapidly between those who are likely, and those who are unlikely to prosecute the study with success, the new system shall release the latter class, after the preliminary year of instruction; 5th, in the former class, *i.e.* those who continue Verse-making, it shall produce nearly, if not quite, as good technical results as if they had spent three times the labour on it; 6th, instead of running the risk of injuring the pupil's English style by recourse to hybrid exercises, the new method shall teach Latin Verse by means of English Verse, by directing the attention to the characteristics of the best English poetry, and creating or developing the germs of a literary taste.

Let us, then, imagine ourselves in the presence of our class, some 25 boys, from 13 to 17 years of age, all of whom have read a book of Virgil, and not less than 300 or 400 lines of Ovid. It will be better, and the teacher's task will be far easier, if they have read more (for a scanty vocabulary is a deficiency that cannot be compensated by any skill in the teacher or intelligence in the pupil), but I assume the very low standard with which experience has made me practically acquainted. If the pupils have not as yet learned any Ovid by heart, they must now begin to learn some. Not much must be learned, but what is learned must be learned well, repeated again and again, till they are quite familiar with it. This is necessary in order that the teacher and pupils may have some common store-house from which to draw materials for the forthcoming lessons; and consequently the boys ought to know some 200 lines, say the *Raptus Proserpinae*, so well as to be able to go on at any passage, and to understand the slightest allusion made to it by the teacher.

As to the prosody, little or no learning of rules will be necessary, if the boys use the pronunciation recommended by the Professors of Oxford and Cambridge, at the request of the Head-masters of schools, some ten years ago. I do not mean to say that mistakes of quantity will not occur, for, as soon as boys begin to write, they will often ignore the most familiar facts of pronunciation, just as they will also ignore the rules of prosody; but I believe the new pronunciation is a great help to us; and whenever I hear, at the performance of a Latin play in a celebrated Public School, "ego" pronounced "eego", I often feel disposed to feel thankful that, in the present keen competition for University distinctions, our formidable rivals are handicapped by the burden of an ancient tradition, which only an ancient school can afford to bear.

But to return to our class. We tell them that we are intending to learn how to write Latin poetry, beginning with Elegiacs, and imitating, as far as we can, the style of Ovid. But, before we begin, do we know what poetry is, and how it differs from prose? There may be some difference, we admit, between English poetry and Latin poetry, of which we may have to treat hereafter; but for the present we ask, What is the object of poetry as distinct from the object of prose? From their English manual, the pupils have an answer ready, and they answer that, while the primary object of ordinary prose is to give information, the primary object of poetry is to give pleasure (where pleasure, it must be admitted, is used in a wide sense). From this general principle, we infer the characteristics of poetic diction. For hence, our pupils tell us,—still quoting from their manual, which they have studied in their English lessons,—poetry often avoids colloquial words and prefers words with old and venerable associations; hence, also, it delights in picturesque expressions; hence, also, it is euphonious; hence, lastly, brief though it is in the cement and grammatical structure of the sentence, it is ample in ornament and imagery. All this may be summed up in the dictum of Milton, that poetry is to be "simple, sensuous, and passionate,"—where it will be explained that the epithet "sensuous" means "appealing readily to the senses," and is applicable to the picturesque images and the euphonious diction of poetry.

Starting, then, from Milton's first epithet, we find that, if poetry is to be "simple" in thought, it must avoid small and subtle distinctions, modifications, qualifications. It will not stand too nicely on arithmetic: the prosaic fact may be that 9999 soldiers fell, but the simplicity of poetry necessitates hyperbole and requires "ten thousand".

Again, since poetry is to be simple in language, it avoids conjunctions of cause, obstacle, result, consequence, and prefers participles and other equivalents,—partly for brevity, but partly from the poetic habit of looking at occurrences in a simple and objective manner. In order to illustrate this for the class, it will be well to turn a few couplets of Ovid into periodic Ciceronian prose, and to bid them note what poor stuff it becomes in the process.

We come now to the second part of Milton's definition. Since poetry is to be "sensuous", that is, to appeal to the ear, it is consequently to be euphonious in diction. Here illustrations from English poetry may be largely employed, and the results of English training may be utilised. In the class which I have in my mind, simultaneously with the commencement of Latin Verse Composition, the study of Pope is commenced; and few English authors bring home to boys the use of euphony so simply and directly as Pope. In their repetition lessons they will naturally commit to memory the famous passages in the Essay on Criticism, which instruct the young poet to adapt his verse to the speed of Camilla, or the slow strength of Ajax; but it is the indirect influence of Pope that will be most useful. It will be good practice for the teacher to read a hundred lines of Pope aloud, previously prepared by the class; and, pausing every now and then, either to leave a blank in the verse, or, better still sometimes, to insert a word of his own which satisfies the metre but is deficient in euphony or exactness, calling upon them to substitute the right word. I have found this a very interesting and stimulating lesson; and its indirect influence has been very marked in teaching boys to distinguish between fit and unfit epithets, and in giving them a perception of euphony.

Applying these results to Latin Verse, we shall have to point out a difference between Latin and English euphony. The history of English poetry shows that initial alliteration was a recognised necessity in the earliest times, and the latent necessity of it still abides with us. In Latin it was not so, and the alliteration, though necessary, is much more artfully concealed, and depends more upon the interior syllables of words; moreover, the alliterative syllables are more often separated from one another with a "wanton head and giddy cunning", which produces a more pleasing effect than the open and brazen-faced repetition of similar sounds. Even in English poetry the necessity for disguised alliteration is now recognised, and the teacher may compare the lines satirised by Shakespeare,—

> The preyful princess pierced and pricked a pretty pricket,

or

> Whereat with blade, with bloody, blameful blade,
> He bravely broached his boiling, bloody breast,

with the disguised and alternate alliteration of the beautiful line in which Milton tells us how, during the passage of the cranes, the air

> Floats as they pass, fann'd with unnumbered plumes.

With such a preparation the pupil will be better prepared to note the alliterations in his Ovidian repetition—

> Terra tribus scopulis vastum procurrit in aequor,
> Trinacris a positu nomen adepta loci;

or the repetition of initial vowels in—

> Valle sub umbrosa locus est aspergine multa
> Uvidus ex alto desilientis aquae.

A teacher might easily give his pupils mechanical rules for constructing a sonorous Latin verse; but such knowledge would probably be worse than worthless, leading them to think more of sound than sense, and tending to mannerism of the worst sort. Much better, occasionally repeat to them lines of striking euphony, and leave them to draw their own inferences, or rather to feel their way towards the best means for producing the full-sounding effect of a solemn line:

> Di, quibus imperium est animarum, umbraeque silentes.
> Monstrum, horrendum, informe, ingens, cui lumen ademtum.
> Non exorando stant adamante fores.
> Porta adversa ingens, solidoque adamante columnae.

We now pass from the sensuousness of poetic language to the sensuousness of poetic thought. Since poetry is to be sensuous, it must be picturesque, avoiding all expressions that do not readily call up images, and preferring particular terms to general abstractions. "Go, lovely rose," for example, is more picturesque, and therefore more effective, than "Go, lovely flower"; and in the *Allegro*, apart from the mischief to the rhythm, you would spoil the poetic picture by substituting "small tree" for "hawthorn", in the couplet which describes how

> Every shepherd tells his tale
> Under the hawthorn in the dale.

This precept of picturesqueness and vividness applies more or less to all poetry, but still more to Latin poetry than to English. In Latin poetry not so much can be left as in English to imagination, and there is less scope for that indirect method of expression which may be described as *innuendo*. "Who is *she?*" would be the question of a Roman, if you began a poem with—

> *She* dwelt among the untrodden ways,

or

> *Her* tears fell with the dews of even.

For this reason you point out that the pronouns "is" and "ea" are hardly ever used in Latin poetry; and, in the two lines above quoted, either nouns or names must be substituted for "she" and "her", even the emphatic form of the pronoun "illa" being impermissible.

It will be quite to the point to explain to our class why Latin poetry must be more definite and distinct than English poetry, especially the poetry of this century. When glancing at subtle changes of the human mind,—many of which have received a prominence in modern times from the influence of our religion,—and when singing of the varied phenomena of nature, of which our poets speak in abstract terms, the ancients recognised the influences of gods and goddesses, Pan, Silvanus, Dryads, Naiads, and the like; and the same tendency to personification runs all through Latin poetry, even where there is no direct mythological influence at work. Hence Croesus represents "the rich"; Pactolus, "wealth"; Niobe, "sorrow for the dead", and so on. To take an extreme case, suppose we have to render in Latin verse the lines of the poet mourning for the loss of a friend in heaven:—

> And our sorrow may cease to repine
> When we know that thy God is with thee,

it has always seemed to me that the audacious rendering which briefly expresses this by an allusion to the story of Ariadne transported to the sky, although it may possibly pass the bounds of good taste, supplies, nevertheless, a most instructive instance of the difference between English and Latin verse: "it is useless to mourn Ariadne, now a constellation in the skies,"—"fletur inutiliter fixa Ariadna polo."

For a similar reason, English abstractions must often be rendered by Latin similes. Thus, in the poem on Epimenides, telling us how the inspired seer put to shame the teachers of conventionalities, it is said that—

> The worldly-wise
> Shrank from the gaze of truth with baffled eyes.

Pierce to the bottom of this, and it seems to mean that the owl-like teachers of common-places shrink from the prophet who soars eagle-like to the sun of truth; and, accordingly, this modern metaphor seems to demand as its Latin equivalent some simile to this effect—

> ——— timidae sic alta petentem
> Bubones aquilam, caeca caterva, tremunt.

Here it may be pointed out that, whereas metaphors, that is to say compressed similes, are appropriate to prose, poetry—and more especially Latin poetry—prefers the simile at full length. The reason is readily deduced from the definition of poetry and its object. The primary object of poetry being to please, it has more leisure for these figures of speech which contribute to pleasure. Besides, a simile is more ancient and simple than metaphor (which is but simile compressed by constant use), and therefore poetry, being both simple and archaic, naturally prefers the simile; and Latin poetry, being more simple and ancient than English poetry, manifests this preference still more strongly than English poetry. It must be added, that many metaphors, which have become so embedded in our language (in poetry as well as prose), that they are scarcely recognized as metaphors, do not admit of being translated literally into Latin. All the more necessary is it that Latin poetry should utilise its natural compensations, viz. simile, personification, and allusion.

Two other minor consequences follow from the picturesqueness of poetry. In the first place, since poetry is to be picturesque, it will indulge more freely than prose in picturesque epithets,—"the red gold," "the blue sky," "the green pastures,"—which are sometimes merely ornamental epithets, as in English Ballad poetry, but at other times serve as simpler substitutes for more complex constructions, such as "the redness of gold," "the blue of the sky," &c. In the next place, since adverbs cannot be picturesque, poetry must substitute for adverbs adverbial phrases which shall appeal to the senses; and hence the bird and the ship will not move "quickly" in verse, but the one "with rapid pinions", the other "with full sail"; the lark also will not always sing "in the morning", but "when the sun rises", and so on.

We come now to the third division in our definition. Poetry, we say, is to be passionate. That is, it must not be scientifically impartial in its statement of facts, but must dwell here with a lighter touch, here with a heavier, tinging everything that it describes with the emotion of some transient thought. For the purposes of a teacher, a good example of the "passionateness" of Latin poetry is to be found in the poetic preference of "jam" to "nunc". It impresses boys to learn how it is that "nunc" (which means "at this present moment," say 2.30 p.m., without regard to past or future) is hardly ever used by Latin poets (except, of course, with imperatives) in comparison with "jam", which means "already" or "at last". With the poets everything happens either sooner, or else later, than might have been hoped or feared. The lingering spring comes "at last"; death comes "already"; in either case "jam", not "nunc". Thus even the colourless element of time, and so passionless a thing as chronology, become tinged, even in Latin elegiacs, with the unscientific "passion" of the poet.

In many different shapes the passion of poetry manifests itself; but one of the most important is the abhorrence of what may be called the enumerative style. Here is a point on which the teacher of boys must lay great stress. Only those who have taught Latin Verse-making to beginners will realise the liability of the boyish mind to this prosaic danger. Strange perverseness! Give a boy a proposition of Euclid to write out, and he will, not unfrequently, explore new paths of fancy, and invent original varieties with startling success: but give him two or three verses to write, say about the seasons of the year, and he will imitate with fatal precision the scientific monotony of the great Geometrician, with results sometimes such as these:—

> Ver venit, atque aestas, exinde auctumnus, hiemsque.

As an antidote against this disease, it is necessary to show one's younger pupils that poetry is worth nothing, unless it is tinged with emotion. But a general precept of this kind is sure to be forgotten, unless impressed by an example, such as the following contrast between Thomson's description of the birds' song-time in spring, and a similar description contained in Sheridan's *Critic*. Here are Thomson's lines:—

> The blackbird whistles from the thorny brake;
> The mellow bullfinch answers from the grove;
> Nor are the linnets, o'er the flowering furze
> Poured out profusely, silent.   *   *   *
>   *   *   The jay, the rook, the daw;
> And each harsh pipe, discordant heard alone,
> Aid the full concert; while the rock-dove breathes
> A melancholy murmur through the whole.

Contrast this with the comical effect of the enumerative style in Sheridan:—

> Now too, the feather'd warblers tune their notes
> Around, and charm the listening grove. The lark,
> The linnet, chaffinch, bullfinch, goldfinch, greenfinch.

Of the two extracts the latter, as far as my experience goes, is more efficacious, as a deterrent, than the former, as an attraction; and the word "chaffinch", scored upon a copy of Latin verses, may convey a criticism brief but more intelligible and impressive than a more lengthy comment.

At this stage, a useful word may be taught in season concerning tautology. For, in teaching boys that tautology (except when it is used for emphasis, or in a refrain) is an offence in poetry, it becomes needful to explain to them why it is not an offence in ordinary prose. Poetry, they must be reminded, does not aim at communicating information, but at infusing thoughts, or at painting a picture in words; and a poet's thought ought not to repeat itself twice in precisely the same way, nor ought a poet's picture to be monotonous. At the present time, it is most important to lay stress on this great difference between poetry and ordinary prose, because the dislike of tautology, spreading from our newspaper-writers, has infected the whole of the nation, to such an extent that sensible men of business, drawing up a business document, will hesitate sometimes to use a most essential word, "man", for example, because, say they, "it has occurred once in this page already[1]". If this should seem a digression, let it be remembered that it is part of our system in teaching Latin Verse Composition to let fall, so to speak, copious crumbs of instruction for the majority who are never likely to write Latin verses well; and it will be a very substantial crumb indeed, that they should, however

[1] The horror of tautology felt by writers for the press is manifested not only in descriptions of prize-fights and races, but even in the details of the Court Circular, and sometimes grapples most skilfully with the driest statistics. Witness the following feat of verbal versatility extracted from the *Times*, of Easter Tuesday, 1882:—"The Botanical Gardens at Kew had their 56,000 visitors against 43,000 last year. The National Gallery, in Trafalgar Square, was visited by 23,700 persons, a number which compares favourably with the 17,283 visitors of 1881. The British Museum received 15,685 visitors between the hours of 10 and 5, a notable advance upon the 10,668 sightseers recorded on the previous Easter Monday."

indirectly, be made to understand that, in the ordinary prose of business, tautology is sometimes as necessary as in Euclid.

But now to recur to Latin Verse-making. After our pupils have obtained some rational notions of the characteristics of poetry, and the causes of them, they will not be harmed by a few hints on the mechanism of Latin Elegiacs.

The first thing to point out is, that each couplet is generally independent of the couplet before and after it; so that the Periodic structure of prose is out of place, and simple sentences must often be used, broken by short parentheses:

> Tota domus laeta est; hoc est, materque paterque,
> Nataque; tres illi tota fuere domus.

Or, again,—

> "Mater," ait virgo,—mota est Dea nomine matris—
> "Quid facis in solis incomitata jugis?"

We then show that the emphasis falls naturally on the end of the pentameter, which place is consequently almost always reserved for some word either emphatic or at all events essential to the sentence. Hence ornamental adjectives, and still more necessarily adverbs, are excluded; and we can place here nothing but verbs, nouns, and essential adjectives (such as the pronominal adjectives *meus*, *tuus*, &c.).

"Now," say we, "let us examine more minutely the words that come at the end of the pentameter. Open your Ovids at the 'Raptus Proserpinae'. You observe that the pentameter ends with an iamb, sometimes beginning with a vowel, sometimes with a consonant. Read out the iambs beginning with a vowel or *h*,—each boy, one." They begin:—*aquae, humus, amant, equis, equi, ubi est, humum, aquas, habet, Eryx, Ityn, humus, aquas, aquae,* &c. You then point out how small is the number of these vowel-iambics, how frequently they recur, and how useful it must be for the purposes of verse-making to have these words at command. You also show how many large classes of words can precede these vowel-iambics, and cannot precede consonant-iambics. Afterwards the boys read out the consonant-iambics in the same way,—*loci, solo, dapes, pede, sinus, labor, sinus, comas, legit, comes, sinus, veni, manus, comis,*—thereby discovering that, although there are three or four times as many of these as of the vowel-iambics, yet even these are limited and soon recur.

You then ask a boy near the bottom how he can turn into a pentameter, "Thus she comes to the Attic harbours." Where in the verse can "Atticos" stand? When even the bottom boy has firmly grasped the discovery that it can stand nowhere, you take this as a text on which you enforce the proposition that Latin differs from English in having a very large number of unmanageable forms of words, which must be altogether excluded from poetry, not as being prosaic, but as being incompatible with the metre. In English this is hardly ever the case, and although some of our longer words (such as "unquestionably") could not find a place in trisyllabic poetry, there is hardly any word in the language that might not, so far as metre is concerned, find a place in the ordinary disyllabic metre. Hence arises the need of certain shifts and devices which are essential for the writer of Latin elegiacs. If we wish to make the goddess "come to the Attic harbours", *Atticos, Atticae,* and *Atticam* being impermissible, we are driven to "Attica" and to apostrophe:

> Sic venit ad portus, Attica terra, tuos.

Mannerisms being thus a necessity in the elegiac metre, we may now fairly point out the use of a few typical phrases, such as "te veniente," "non valiturus," "qui fuit ante," "non sine," and leave the pupils, in the course of their reading, to make further discoveries of typical phrases for themselves. Collecting these phrases in a rational way, with a clear insight into the artificial structure of the Latin elegiac, and with the reflection constantly suggesting itself to him, "How different this is from English poetry!" it need not be feared lest our pupils should be intellectually demoralized by an hour or two spent in the analysis of the elegiac metre. But everything should be done at first with the guidance of the teacher, and *viva voce* in class; no homework being as yet given, for fear the pupil should fall into bad slow habits, or be discouraged because he is retarded by a scanty vocabulary. In this way the drudgery of tags and ends and beginnings of verses, which often occupies boys for a month or more, may be got through in two or three hours, and with better results than those attained by the slow system.

Having now described our preliminary lessons on the nature of poetry in general, and on the mechanism of Latin elegiacs in particular, we proceed to apply our theories to practice by writing Latin verses. It seems to me the best plan that the first two or three exercises should be on "skeleton subjects", if they may be so called, allowing the boys a very ample latitude in construction and even in thought. Thus, let our English be:—

> The hawk
> Looks down on the birds.

"What is the thought here implied? How is the hawk regarded in his relation to the birds?"—"As a conqueror, oppressor, king, &c." "What epithets, then, will suit the hawk?"—"Swift, cruel, high up, proud, lordly, king of the birds, &c." "What epithet will suit the birds?"—"Small, timid, silent, unwarlike." "How shall we make the hawk picturesque?" One boy suggests that he is to be represented "high up"; another, "with poised wings"; another, "looking down from a high rock". Out of a kind of struggle between this multitude of suggestions having secured the survival of the fittest, we proceed to business. "What word will come at the end of the pentameter?"—"Aves." "And before 'aves'?"—"Altus." "Well, let us try it; what will come then before 'altus'?"—"Despicit." "True, and now you might make a seventh-rate line by adding that he looks down from 'the liquid air above'; how would the verse run?"—"Aethere de liquido despicit altus aves." "Now tell me why is this line a poor one." Silence. "What does 'aethere de liquido' tell you?"—"Where the hawk is." "And what does 'altus' tell you?"—"Where the hawk is." "Then why is the verse poor?"—"Because it repeats the same thing in different words." We now have the Ovids opened, and find that in the vast majority of cases the noun coming at the end of the pentameter has an epithet to prepare the way for it, partly because poetry dislikes surprises, partly to express some thought or suggest some picture. Recurring to our store of epithets, we obtain, perhaps,

Despicit, en, timidas aethere celsus aves.

Objecting to the particle "en" introduced before "timidas," as being unnecessary, we obtain, as an amendment, "imbelles." Still we are not contented. We remind the class that in their English manual, which gives them suggestions for writing clearly and forcibly, there is a certain element mentioned as tending to force and point, which is—? "Antithesis." "How are we to obtain antithesis?"—"By attaching to 'hawk' an epithet antithetical to 'imbelles'." Making trial of this, perhaps the same boy who suggested "en timidas," now suggests "ecce, superbus"; but, being emphatically remonstrated with for his love of expletives, and the class having been solemnly warned that the introduction of "ecce," "en," "jam," and the like, is fatal to progress, if boys fall back upon that expedient whenever it can make a line scan, he gives place to better thoughts, and the class is led to see that a full-sounding word signifying "lordly, imperious," will be appropriate here, ultimately lighting on "imperiosus":

"Despicit imbelles imperiosus aves."

The same process will now have to be repeated with the hexameter, except that, whereas he always began with the last word of the pentameter, the teacher's first question, in dealing with the hexameter, will be, "What word or words will come naturally at the beginning?" He will then show the boys how to adapt the end of the hexameter, so as to connect it smoothly with the pentameter; and he will teach them, above all things, to keep their minds open to new thoughts, new images, and new expressions,—not binding themselves fast down to one beginning or end, which may be found incompatible with a happy rendering of the whole couplet, but tossing, as it were, in their minds a number of thoughts, and evolving, out of their mutual conflict, a survival of the fittest.

In this lesson, the teacher will do wisely not to lay down

always beforehand what shape the verses shall take, but to catch up any hints the class may give, and to follow them out as far as possible; sometimes so as to make the worst of them, exhibiting clearly the fault inherent in the original suggestion; but at other times making the best of them, even though it may be impossible to make that best into anything very good. For it must be remembered that boys are often less interested, and often learn less, in hearing first-rate verses that come to them perfect from the teacher's lips—perfect and hopelessly inimitable—than they learn from second or third-rate verses, over the making of which they have watched or even participated. It may be third-rate; but the boy's heart says feelingly, with Touchstone, "A poor thing, sir, but mine own".

After two or three exercises of this kind, it will be time to give the class a copy of simple English verses to turn into Latin. And here all that I would urge is,—(1) that the English verses shall have in them a little poetry; (2) that they shall not be accompanied by any Latinized English version, which, if allowed, is fatal to all thought about the English poem, and to any originality in rendering it; the boys being sensible enough to know that the Latinized version makes the English superfluous, and far too modest, or too lazy, to prefer thinking for themselves when they have an interpreter to do the thinking for them.

As to the way in which these new exercises should be attempted, there is little to add to what has been said above, except that, in starting, the first question will always be, What is the poet's thought? By which we do not mean What is the literal meaning of the first few words? but What is the thought running through the whole poem? Is he sad? Joyful? Hopeful? Despairing? Wondering?

Loving? Hating? The turn of every expression throughout the poem may be influenced by the answer. For, suppose you have to render and to amplify, "the sun was setting". Obviously, the poet may be regarding sunset in a pleasing aspect ("the departing sun was bringing welcome rest to men"), or in a gloomy aspect ("the sun was fleeing before sad darkness"). And we must point out to the class how more especially the opening words of the translation must be carefully adapted to express in rhythm, as well as in thought, the purpose of the original, because they serve as a kind of key-note to prepare the mind and ear for what is to come afterwards. A good illustration may be obtained by the contrast between the sad monotony and the sprightly variety of the two following openings:—

> When I consider how my life is spent,
> Ere half my days, in this dark world and wide.

> Now the bright morning-star, day's harbinger,
> Comes dancing from the East, and brings with her
> The flowery May.

The rest of the lesson will consist of the application of the principles laid down above; and only a few hints need be added.

1. Do not severely snub effervescence and exuberance; but remember the dictum of the great orator: "Velim effervescat atque exuberet juventus."

2. Be always prepared with a few amusing English examples of poetic errors, so as to illustrate the faults of the young composers in an interesting and impressive way. "The Critic" and "Rejected Addresses" will generally supply you with instances. Tameness, for example, and platitudes, are appropriately censured by reference to the

hackney-coach drawn by those well-known horses of which the poet assures us that—

> The tails of both hung down behind,
> Their shoes were on their feet,

or by quoting the lines which tell how—

> John Edward William Alexander Dwyer
> Was footman to Justinian Stubbs, Esquire.

In order, however, that these castigations may be effective, it is necessary that these or similar passages should have been read, or committed to memory, by the class in their English lesson. I cannot think that the time spent in such a task will be wasted. The class I have in my mind is in the habit of committing to memory a stanza of eight lines, illustrating the not uncommon habit of sacrificing sense to sound. It begins by describing how—

> 'Tis sweet to roam when morning's light
> Resounds across the deep,

and ends with a couplet which I have never found a boy capable of forgetting:

> And the wolf rings out with a glittering shout
> To-whit, to-whit, to-whoo!

"What rubbish!"—some of my younger auditors may possibly feel inclined to say—"what rubbish to make boys learn by heart!" Yes, I reply, but what rubbish, what very similar rubbish, at this very time, is written and even published, not in Latin verses merely, but in English, and not by boys only, but even by those older than boys, and under the guise of poetry too, by some who have enjoyed or are enjoying the advantages of being educated at this or at the sister University! To my mind, these eight lines of rubbish are a possession for ever for the youthful mind, never likely to be more precious than in the present generation.

Some conscientious and scholarlike teachers may be deterred from giving such a lesson as I have been attempting to describe above, because such verses as will be the outcome of it, appear to them less profitable to their pupils, and less satisfactory to their own self-respect, than those which they could elaborate in the evening solitude, with pains and thought, to be presented to their class on the following morning as a "fair copy". Such scruples are certainly misplaced. If the class contributes its fair share of suggestions, the boys, and not the teacher, may be considered responsible for the verses; and, so far from feeling obliged to assume that they are excellent, part of the teacher's duty will be to point out the defects of the couplet when the best has been made of it, and to assume that the joint-stock method of verse-writing seldom results in the highest felicitousness. Besides, when the class has done its best, the teacher can always, if he likes, produce some elaborate and excellent translation with which the boys can contrast their own.

But, should the teacher avail himself of such a translation, I should strongly advise him not to look at it, or know anything of it, till he reads it out to his class. Otherwise, he cannot so readily place himself on a level with his boys. The very beauties of the translation, striking his fancy and continually recurring to his mind, will preoccupy him to the exclusion of other inferior renderings, and will prevent him from accepting the suggestions of his pupils, and from following out each train of thought as far as it will lead him. Not having any problems himself to solve, he will not be so well able to appreciate the difficulties of the class in their attempts to solve them. Besides, it takes away a great deal of the stimulus of the lesson, when the teacher no longer feels himself on his mettle, genuinely working at the same questions which are perplexing his class. To the boys, also, there is a diminution of the interest, when they feel that the master has an unfair advantage over them in the possession of what they may profanely call "a crib". Therefore, if the teacher has pluck enough for it, it is best that the *Foliorum Silvula* should be opened at manifest random, so that all the class may perceive that master and boys together are entering on unknown regions, in a common voyage of exploration.

After nearly a year's work of this kind, the teacher will be able, without difficulty, to make three divisions in his class,—1st, the majority, who have neither taste, memory, nor knowledge enough, to enable them to prosecute this study by themselves; 2nd, those who would like to continue it, and are so far qualified for it that they may be permitted to prosecute it for a year longer, on probation; 3rd, the very small minority, who have a distinct taste for it, and who (at all events in the present condition of studies at the Universities) may be encouraged to attempt to attain skill in it, at the heavy cost of two or three hours a week. For these, as well as for the second class, little more can be done by oral teaching. They must now be left to depend on their own reading, aided only by the criticism of their exercises, and the occasional comparison of their own verses with good "originals".

At one point, however, effectual assistance may be given to them; and that is when they are first introduced to hexameters. Boys mostly approach this new metre, under the illusion that it is not new. Whereas, before, they wrote a hexameter first, and a pentameter second, now they vainly suppose that they are to make both lines hexameters, and the same hexameters as before. They do not know that, in the first place, the unmixed hexameter implies a continuous style, not broken into couplets and not admitting a regular pause at the end of the line; and that, in the second place, when we speak of hexameters, we mean Virgilian hexameters, as different from Ovid's, as Milton's blank verse is from Pope's couplets,—a hexameter in which the pause, not at the end of the line, but at different positions in the line, is as important an element as it is in the *Paradise Lost;* and that hexameters without pauses, and carefully varied pauses, are not worthy to be called hexameters at all. The following passage from the seventh book of the *Paradise Lost*, previously committed to memory in an English lesson, for the purpose of enforcing the beauty of the pause in English blank verse, may well be repeated at this stage:—

> From branch to branch the smaller birds with song
> Solaced the woods, | and spread their painted wings
> Till even; || nor then the solemn nightingale
> Ceased warbling, | but all night tuned her soft lays.||
> Others, || on silver lakes and rivers, | bathed
> Their downy breast; || the swan with arched neck
> Between her white wings mantling proudly, | rows
> Her state with oary feet; || yet oft they quit
> The dank, | and rising with stiff pennons, tower
> The mid aerial sky.||

After this, some passages must be selected from Virgil, to show the subtle art with which the Virgilian hexameter avoids monotony, by varying, not only the pause, but also the subject, and the position of the subject; and how he combines the continuous and periodic structure, fit for the higher level of elevated poetry, with the more abrupt verse which suits graphic narrative on a lower level. The contrast between *Æneid* I. 1—11, in the elevated and continuous style, and the following lines in the abrupt style, beginning "urbs antiqua fuit," would furnish a good instance, but are too long to quote. Let us take the opening of the sixth book, where two continuous lines with one subject describe Æneas smoothly sailing into the coast of Cumæ, and then follow six lines with six several subjects in every variety of position:

> Sic fatur lacrimans, classique immittit habenas,
> Et tandem Euboicis Cumarum adlabitur oris.
> Obvertunt pelago proras; tum dente tenaci
> Ancora fundabat naves; et littora curvae
> Praetexunt puppes. Juvenum manus emicat ardens
> Littus in Hesperium; quaerit pars semina flammae
> Abstrusa in venis silicis, pars densa ferarum
> Tecta rapit, silvas, inventaque flumina monstrat.

Even with all this telling and warning, the necessary effect will not yet have been produced. It will, therefore, be a good plan, when the first copy of hexameters is set, to bid the young composers select some passage in Virgil, as similar in thought as they can find to the English before them, and to reproduce the pauses of that Virgilian passage. If they still altogether neglect or fail to do this, the copy must be torn up, and they must do it again, or give up the attempt to write in this metre; but in no case must the teacher allow himself to tolerate, or take the trouble of correcting, a copy of pauseless hexameters.

One word of warning in conclusion. We have been dealing with a class of some 25 boys, of whom not one, or not more than one, is under 14 years of age at the time of commencing our course; and our materials had to be drawn from one book of Virgil, and 500 lines of Ovid. It must not be expected that even the best specimens of such a class, beginning with so small a vocabulary, and so slight a knowledge of Latin poetry, will equal the very best performances of those who begin verse-writing and verse-learning from the age of 10 or 11. But the best of those taught on the short system will rapidly overtake and surpass all but the very best of those who have learned on the long system; and I am inclined to think that, with more reading and a larger vocabulary, they could not be prevented by the late commencement of actual verse-making from reaching even the highest results achieved by the early verse-writers. But the teacher who should try this method must not expect too much at first. Let it be remembered, that there is to be no home-work at first; and even afterwards not more than half an hour a week is to be compulsory. Not much can be done by a slow boy, in the way of thoughtful and rational verse-writing, in half an hour. The great majority will produce practically nothing. Yet the teacher ought not to consider the time wasted if the dull pupil gives evidence of having applied his mind to the task. Better one poor, one very poor couplet, with traces of thought, than thirty mechanically evolved correct verses. For the majority of the class, let it be never forgotten, the object of teaching Latin verses is, not that they may write Latin verses, but that they may attain some degree of literary taste and judgment. Whether this object might be better attained directly by teaching English verse composition, than indirectly by teaching Latin verse composition, is another question, into which there is no space to enter. For myself, I shrink from this alternative, regarding the mother-tongue as too sacred a material to trifle with in the same venturesome way in which one makes and re-makes a Latin elegiac, and shrinking from the irretrievable injury that an incisive lesson on the art of writing English poetry might possibly inflict on some future Shelley or Shakespeare. In any case, I submit to your consideration this sketch of an attempt to teach Latin verse through English verse, with at least one ground of confidence. It may be defective,—it may be bad,—it may be even very bad,—and yet it may be a great deal better than the present system.

www.ingramcontent.com/pod-product-compliance
Lightning Source LLC
Chambersburg PA
CBHW030411170426
43202CB00010B/1571